creating a photo album
in photoshop elements
for windows

Visual QuickProject Guide

by Katherine Ulrich

**Peachpit
Press**

Visual QuickProject Guide
Creating a Photo Album in Photoshop Elements for Windows
Katherine Ulrich

Peachpit Press
1249 Eighth Street
Berkeley, CA 94710
510/524-2178
800/283-9444
510/524-2221 (fax)

Find us on the World Wide Web at: www.peachpit.com
To report errors, please send a note to errata@peachpit.com
Peachpit Press is a division of Pearson Education

Copyright © 2005 by Katherine Ulrich

Editor: Nancy Davis
Production Editor: Lisa Brazieal
Compositor: Katherine Ulrich
Indexer: Karin Arrigoni
Technical Review: Victor Gavenda
Cover design: The Visual Group with Aren Howell
Interior design: Elizabeth Castro
Interior photos: Katherine Ulrich
Cover photo credit: Photodisc

ISBN 0-321-27081-9

9 8 7 6 5 4 3 2 1

Printed and bound in the United States of America

To my parents, Reva and John,
who shared with me their love of
nature and the joys of observation,
from the very beginning.

Special Thanks to...

Perry Whittle, whose ongoing support, both moral and technical, smoothed out the bumps in the road to writing this book.

David Van Ness, my InDesign guru, for guiding me through the page-layout process.

Victor Gavenda, for combing through these pages for errors and goofs of a technical nature.

Bob Gager, Group Product Manager, Adobe Photoshop Services, for his generous help with my questions about creating albums in Photoshop Elements.

Nancy Davis, my editor, for her consistently upbeat spirit, words of encouragement, and editorial direction.

Lisa Brazieal, for her production expertise and shepherding these pages through the process.

Marjorie Baer, for her friendship and for thinking this project might be for me.

Karin Arrigoni, for creating the book's index on a tight timeline.

San Francisco Botanical Garden at Strybing Arboretum, where most of the photos in this book were taken. I'm grateful to the gardeners, volunteers, and staff, for creating a beautiful living museum of plants, a haven for small creatures of every sort, an oasis of calm in the midst of the bustling city.

contents

contents

introduction

The Visual QuickProject Guide that you hold in your hands offers a unique way to learn about new technologies. Instead of drowning you in theoretical possibilities and lengthy explanations, this Visual QuickProject Guide uses big, color illustrations coupled with clear, concise step-by-step instructions to show you how to complete one specific project in a matter of hours.

Our project in this book is to assemble your digital photos into an album using Adobe Photoshop Elements for Windows. Using the Album Creation wizard in Elements, we'll arrange photos in layouts for printing on a home printer, on high-quality photo paper. You can assemble these pages into albums using three-ring notebooks, portfolio binders, or any cover materials that appeal to you. We'll also use the Album Creation wizard to arrange photos in layouts that you can order as bound hardcover books. In the process, we'll learn about working with Elements Organizer to create catalogs of photos. And we'll learn some basic photo-enhancing techniques using tools in Elements Editor.

Of course, you could always place individual photo prints into commercial albums or homemade scrapbooks. But the Album Creation wizard makes it easy to arrange multiple photos on a single page, and the wizard's templates let you create albums in a variety of styles. There are styles that place photos in special frames, some sophisticated and elegant, others whimsical or theme-based. There are styles that show off the photos on plain white pages. The Album Creation wizard frees you from the drudgery (and in my case, the illegibility) of handwritten captions, making it easy to add high-quality text. Here's another plus: the major work in creating an album is placing the photos on the page. With traditional albums, you must redo that work for each and every album, even if you're just re-creating the same one for different members of your family. In Elements, once the work of creating the album is done, you just print or order the number of copies you need.

what you'll create

Bring your digital photos into Elements Organizer.

Create a catalog structure with categories and tags, then create collections to gather the photos you want to use in your album.

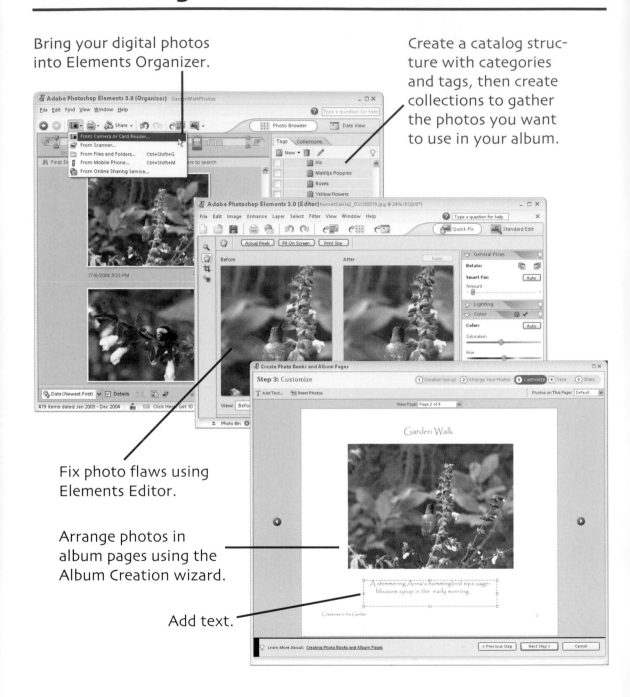

Fix photo flaws using Elements Editor.

Arrange photos in album pages using the Album Creation wizard.

Add text.

Use Adobe Photoshop Services, Provided by Ofoto, to order a hard-cover book printed from your album pages.

Print album pages yourself and create your own binding system.

how this book works

The title explains what is covered in this section.

Orange highlight calls out special terms, names of steps that make up the interface of the Album Creation wizard, and cross references in this book.

Numbers clarify the precise order of steps you need to follow to complete a task.

Dotted arrows show interactive movement, for example, dragging a photo to a new location.

Purple tint connects an area of detail to an enlarged view of that area.

Screenshots illustrate the essential areas of the software interface that you will work with.

put photos in order

You can change the order of your images in Step 2: Arrange Your Photos.

1 Click the photo you want to move, then drag it to a new position. (To move several photos, Ctrl-click each one; if the photos are in a row, click the first one, then Shift-click the last one to select them all. Dragging one photo moves the whole selected group, even if the photos are not contiguous.)

2 The yellow bar highlights the new placement. Release the mouse.

3 The Album Creation wizard reorders the images and reassigns their pages.

creating albums with fixed layouts 61

Captions describe the actions you need to take to complete the task described in the section.

introduction

The extra bits section at the end of each chapter contains additional tips and tricks that you might like to know—but that aren't absolutely necessary for creating your photo album.

The page number that follows the heading helps you find the content area in the main text.

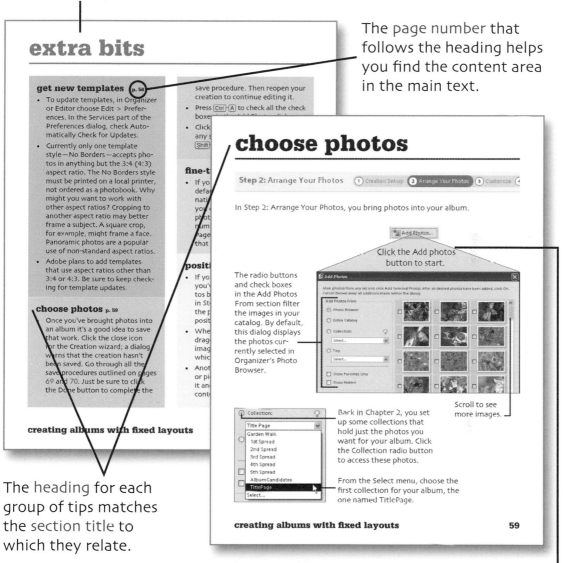

The heading for each group of tips matches the section title to which they relate.

An orange triangle connecting objects indicates cause and effect. Here, clicking the Add Photos button opens the Add Photos dialog.

the next step

This Visual QuickProject Guide gets you started using a variety of tools in Photoshop Elements, but the real focus is on creating photo albums. That means giving short shrift to many of Elements' organizing and editing features. For more in-depth coverage, you might consider adding another book to your library: Photoshop Elements for Windows & Macintosh: Visual QuickStart Guide.

CRAIG HOESCHEN

PHOTOSHOP ELEMENTS
FOR WINDOWS & MACINTOSH

VISUAL QUICKSTART GUIDE

Teach yourself Photoshop ... the quick and easy ... Visual QuickStart ... pictures rather than ... explanations. You'll be ... running in no time!

Figure 3.32 The Shadows/Highlights dialog box.

Figure 3.33 The top photo is a little under-exposed in the foreground, so detail in the young woman's face is hidden in shadow. In the bottom photo, making adjustments with the Lighten Shadows and the Midtone Contrast sliders selectively brightens and enhances detail in both her face and blouse.

Lighting Your Image

Overexposed background images and under-exposed foreground subjects are a common problem for most amateur photographers. Photoshop Elements provides an elegant tool to help salvage your otherwise perfect com-positions. Much like levels, it operates on pixels in specific tonal ranges (either high-lights or shadows) while leaving the other tonal ranges alone. A Lighten Shadows slider helps to add detail to areas in shadow, while a Darken Highlights slider can add detail to washed-out areas in the background.

To improve foreground detail:

1. From the Enhance menu, choose Adjust Lighting > Shadows/Highlights. The Shadows/Highlights dialog box appears (**Figure 3.32**).

2. In the Shadows/Highlights dialog box, drag the Lighten Shadows slider to the right to lessen the effect of the shadows, or to the left to introduce shadow back into the image.

3. Drag the Midtone Contrast slider to the right to increase the contrast, or to the left to decrease the contrast.

4. Click OK to close the Shadows/Highlights dialog box and apply the changes (**Figure 3.33**).

✔ **Tips**

■ I've found that in many (if not most) images imported from a digital camera, the Shadows/Highlights dialog box defaults work surprisingly well on their own, requiring just minor slider adjustments.

■ In any case, use the Midtone Contrast slider sparingly. A little goes a long way, and adjustments of more than plus or minus 10% can quickly wash out or flat-ten an image's details.

85

LIGHTING YOUR IMAGE

The Visual QuickStart Guide teaches you step-by-step how to use Elements to enhance your photos, improving their quality and heightening their impact. Like all of the books in Peachpit's Visual QuickStart Guide series, it also works as a reference guide when you just need to learn (or remember) the steps for com-pleting a task.

introduction

1. getting ready

You've been shooting like mad with your new digital camera, or spending every spare minute scanning old family snapshots. Now you'd like to show off your work and preserve it in a special photo album. You're about to embark on an album-creation project using Adobe Photoshop Elements 3.0 for Windows.

You'll import photos into Elements Organizer; retouch them in Elements Editor; then, using Organizer's Album Creation wizard, arrange them in neat layouts with text. You'll create album pages that can be printed as individual 8.5-by-11-inch pages, using high-quality photo paper, on your own printer. You are free to bind these into an album however you like. For a simple album, punch three holes in each page and put the pages into a three-ring binder from your local Five and Dime. For something a bit fancier, punch just two holes and thread the pages with ribbon or cord. Check local art-supply, crafts, or office-products stores and you'll find many styles of binders, portfolios, and cover materials.

The most luxurious album option is to create layouts for 10.25-by-9-inch pages. Using Adobe Photoshop Services, provided by Ofoto you can order a photobook. Ofoto, a Kodak subsidiary, professionally prints your album pages and binds them into a hardcover book.

general preparations

1 To install Photoshop Elements 3.0 you need

A PC with at least an 800MHz Intel Pentium III or 4 processor (or one that's compatible) and a CD-ROM drive.

Microsoft Windows XP Professional or Home Edition with Service Pack 1; Windows 2000 with Service Pack 4 or later.

At least 256MB of RAM (Adobe recommends 512MB) and 800MB of free space on your hard-drive.

A color monitor and video card capable of handling 16-bit color or greater. (Set your monitor resolution to 1024 by 768 or greater when using Elements.)

2 Calibrate Your Monitor

How do you know that the beautiful colors you see on screen will be the same beautiful colors when you print your photos or album pages or send them out to be printed professionally? Well the truth is, the printed versions will never give you the luminous bright colors you see on your computer monitor. But you can do something to help ensure that your delicate pink rose doesn't come out fire-engine red, and the bright baskets of pollen on a bumblebee's legs are orange not greeny gray. The way to do this is to use color management and to calibrate your monitor. We'll use a simple color-management technique in creating album pages, but monitor calibration is beyond the scope of this book. When you install Elements you also install Adobe Gamma software. The Elements Help feature describes how to use this software to calibrate a CRT monitor. You can also purchase special tools and software specifically for calibrating your monitor. These can get fairly pricey, however, and require devoted attention to achieve the most consistent results.

To run the Adobe Gamma application, use the Windows Start menu to open the Control Panel window. Choose the category named Appearance and Themes. Adobe Gamma is listed with the Control Panel icons. Click the Adobe Gamma icon to start the calibration process.

project materials

1 A digital camera with which to take your photos.

2 A PC computer with Windows.

3 Adobe Photoshop Elements 3.0 for Windows.

4 Adobe Reader for previewing layouts for album pages and hardcover photobooks in Portable Document Format (PDF).

5 A printer. Color ink-jet printers enable you to print your own individual album pages or proof pages in color before ordering a hardcover photobook. Black-and-white printers are good for proofing layouts and text without eating up your stocks of color inks.

6 Low-quality paper for proofing album pages before committing to high-quality paper or ordering a book online.

7 High-quality photo paper for printing finished album pages.

8 An Internet connection for ordering hardcover photobooks through Adobe Photoshop Services, provided by Ofoto.

9 A credit card to complete the online transaction of ordering hardcover photobooks.

project steps

1 Acquire images. For this project, I'll be using photos I shot with a digital camera, but you could just as easily create an album from scans that you've made of older snapshots or documents. You could also use the graphics tools in Elements to create original artwork and use that artwork in your album.

2 Import the photos to Elements Organizer. Organizer is a complete asset-management application within Elements. Organizer keeps track of your photos in a catalog—basically a database of photos.

3 Create structure. You create a hierarchical structure for the database by assigning categories, subcategories, and tags to the photos in the catalog. These structural features work just like keywords in a database, allowing you to identify and ultimately, sort through, your photos. You can filter your catalog to find just the photos you want by asking to see only photos in certain categories or that have certain tags attached.

4 Gather photos for your album. Another quasi-structural feature of Organizer is the collection. A collection is a container (think electronic shoebox) where you can hold a set of photos and arrange them in any order you like.

5 Fix up your photos. No matter how careful you are when shooting in the field, you're bound to take a few shots that could use a little help. Use Elements' editing tools to do such things as crop, fix exposure problems, remove color casts and red-eye syndrome, and retouch minor flaws. Because of a little glitch in the album-creation feature, it's important to edit the photos you want to include in an album before you start creating it. In some cases, editing photos after putting them into an album causes the album to lose all its data.

6 Create album pages. Elements comes with a Creation wizard: a tool that helps you make a variety of printed materials from postcards, to calendars, to our projects—photo album pages and photobooks. Using templates, the Album Creation wizard guides you through the process of creating album pages. These can be printed on your own printer, or sent to a local print shop, or they can be printed professionally and bound into hardcover photobooks.

7 Order a photobook and/or print album pages on high-quality paper designed for your printer, for example, matte or glossy ink-jet photo paper.

getting ready

Elements basics

 To open Elements, double-click its icon on the desktop or choose it from the Windows Start menu.

Elements contains two application areas: Organizer and Editor. Each opens in its own separate work area. Organizer has two viewing modes: Photo Browser and Date View. Editor has two editing modes: Quick Fix and Standard Edit.

Initially, Elements 3.0 opens to the Welcome Screen. This screen is the gateway to all the functional pieces of Elements. Click a button to begin using Elements. The four functions called out below are the ones you'll use in our projects.

Click to open Organizer.

Click to open Editor in Quick Fix mode.

Click to open Editor in Standard mode.

Click to open the Creation wizard.

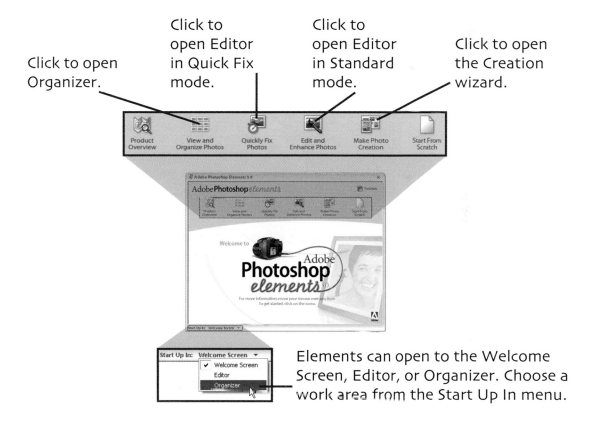

Elements can open to the Welcome Screen, Editor, or Organizer. Choose a work area from the Start Up In menu.

Elements basics (cont.)

1 ORGANIZER

Use Organizer to store and, well, organize your photos. The shortcuts bar offers quick entry to various tasks. Click the appropriate icon to begin.

Import
photos to
catalog
(Chapter 1).

Open Cre-
ation wizard
(Chapters 4
and 5).

Open Editor (Chapter 3).

View photos by
date added to
catalog.

Double-click-
ing photos
toggles
between
the largest
and smallest
thumbnails.

The Organize
Bin shows
your tags and
collections,
the structural
elements of
your catalog
(Chapter 2).

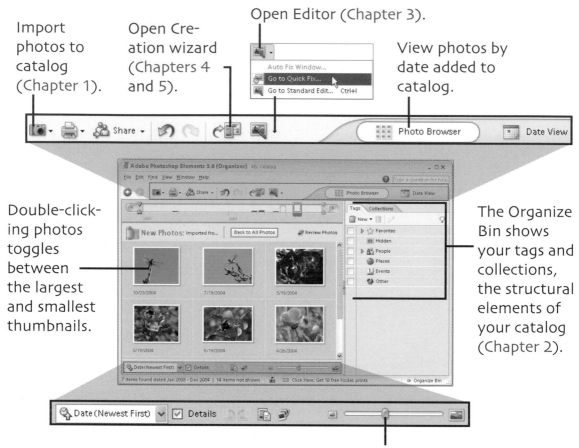

Drag the thumbnail slider to view
thumbnails at intermediate sizes.

getting ready

2 EDITOR

Use Editor in Quick Fix mode to make simple corrections to your photos. Use Editor in Standard Edit mode to make more complex corrections to your photos and create original artwork.

Open Creation wizard (Chapters 4 and 5).

Open Organizer in Photo Browser mode (Chapter 2).

Enter Quick Fix mode (Chapter 3).

Enter Standard Edit mode (Chapter 3).

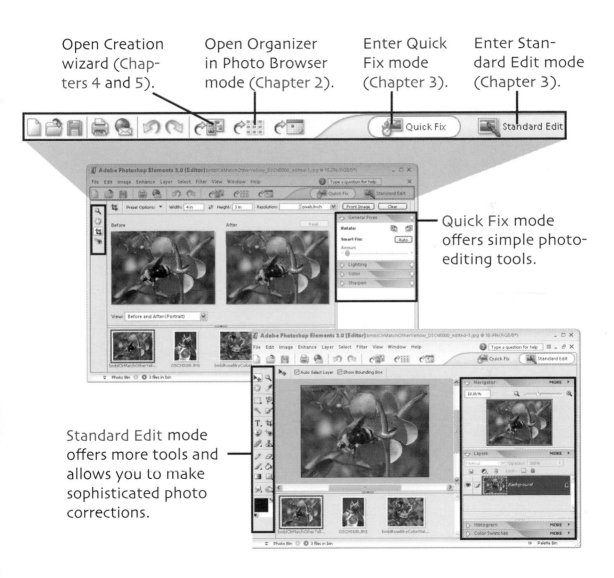

Quick Fix mode offers simple photo-editing tools.

Standard Edit mode offers more tools and allows you to make sophisticated photo corrections.

import photos

There are many ways to get photos into Organizer. You can download photos from a camera or card reader. You can set Elements to download photos automatically when you plug in the camera or insert a memory card into a card reader connected to your PC. You can also grab images that you've downloaded to your hard drive or burned onto CD-ROM. You can set up Watch folders so that any time you add files to a specified folder, Elements grabs them and puts them into Organizer. For this project, I used a card reader.

To start the import process, open Organizer.

Most people use just one catalog, the default My Catalog. If several people, say your whole family, use one computer, you might set up separate catalogs for each user. If you have multiple catalogs, open the one to which you want to add photos. Choose File > Catalog. The Catalog dialog appears.

Click the Open button in the Catalog dialog.

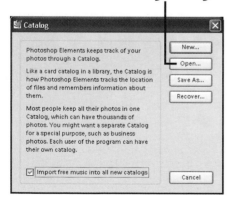

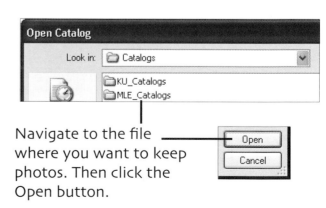

Navigate to the file where you want to keep photos. Then click the Open button.

In Organizer, with your catalog open, click the Get Photos button.

Choose a device or location from the menu.

In the Get Photos from Camera or Card Reader dialog, choose the card reader device.

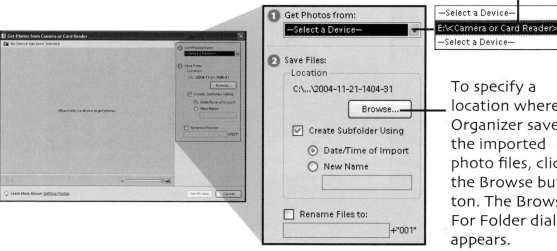

To specify a location where Organizer saves the imported photo files, click the Browse button. The Browse For Folder dialog appears.

In the Browse For Folder dialog, navigate to the folder where you want Organizer to save your photo files.

Click OK to close the dialog.

getting ready

import photos (cont.)

Elements previews the memory card's photos in the Get Photos from Camera or Card Reader dialog.

By default, all images are selected. Click a check box to deselect any photo(s) you don't want to import.

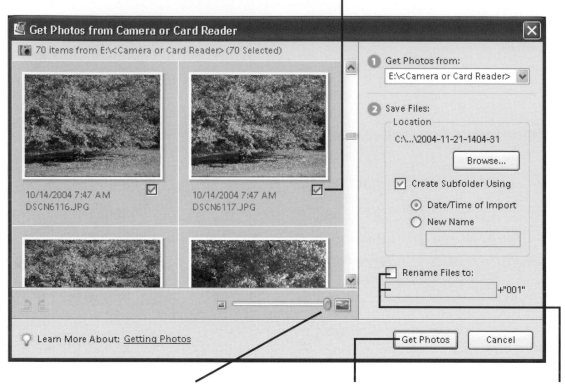

Drag the thumbnail slider to change the size of the preview thumbnail.

Click the Get Photos button to import the selected items to your catalog.

Check the Rename Files To check box and enter a meaningful name for your files. Elements adds sequential numbers at the end of the file name.

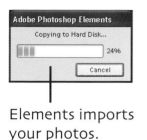

Elements imports your photos.

Elements warns you that the catalog shows just the imported images. To avoid seeing this note, click the Don't Show Again check box.

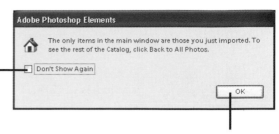

Click OK to close the dialog.

When import is done, you have the option to delete images from your memory card. Click No. It's better to let your camera do the deleting. Plus you can verify that you got all the photos you wanted before deleting them for good.

To display your full catalog, click the Back to All Photos button.

extra bits

general preparations p. 2

- Installing Elements automatically installs Adobe Reader 6.0.1 and Microsoft DirectX 9.0 if you don't already have them installed (these applications are included on the Elements CD).

import photos p. 8

- When Organizer previews the images from your card reader, in the Get Photos from Camera or Card Reader dialog, you can press Ctrl-A to select all the images.

- Press Shift-Ctrl-A to deselect all the images.

- To select noncontiguous photos, Ctrl-click each one.

- To select a range of photos, click the first one, then Shift-click the last one.

2. creating structure within your catalog

Once you start having fun with your digital camera, the number of photos you need to keep track of balloons quickly. Organizer's catalogs are really databases in disguise. Use your catalog to bring order to the chaos of your photo files.

Digital cameras record lots of information for each file, for example, the date and time you took the photo, the format, a file name. Organizer automatically enters that information into your catalog. You can add other details in captions and notes. To make it possible to sort your photos, you add categories, sub-categories, and tags. Finally, you can gather a set of photos for a specific purpose by creating collections and collection groups.

Categories and tags are Organizer's version of searchable keywords, while collections and collection groups act more like electronic shoe boxes storing groups of photos for use in a project. We'll make one collection group and several collections to gather photos for our album. Once you place photos in a collection, you can put them in any order you like. The collection contains links to your photo files. Photos in a collection still appear in their original catalog. Catalog searches still find these photos, and you can add them to other collections for other projects. Using tags, we'll narrow the range of candidates for our album, then gather the finalists into collections for each set of facing pages.

add captions and notes

Click the tiny triangle to close and open the Organize Bin.

1 In the Photo Browser view in Organizer, click a photo to select it.

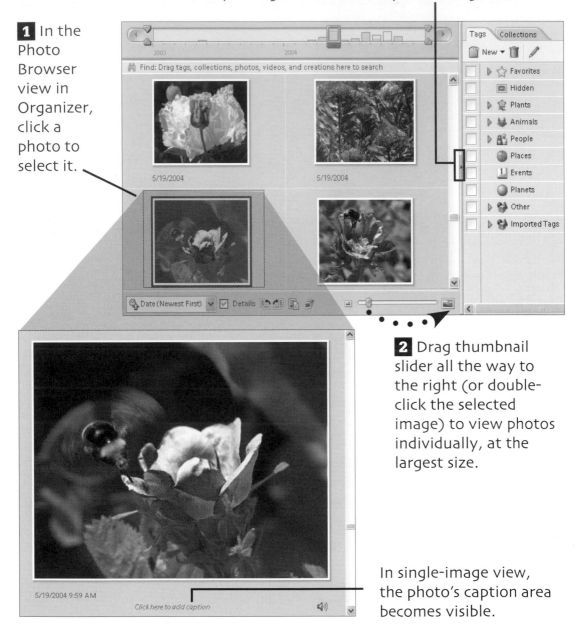

2 Drag thumbnail slider all the way to the right (or double-click the selected image) to view photos individually, at the largest size.

In single-image view, the photo's caption area becomes visible.

3 Click the caption area to activate the text field.

4 Start typing your caption text. Press enter to confirm the caption.

Organizer automatically enters data from your camera, such as a file name and date, into the Properties window.

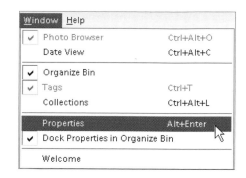

To view the properties of a selected image, choose Window > Properties, or press Alt - Enter. The Properties window opens in the Organize Bin.

The Caption, Name, and Notes fields are all editable.

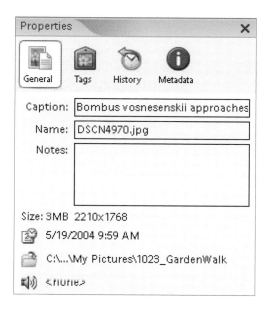

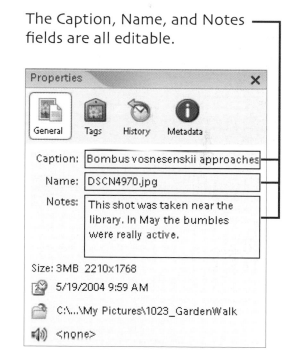

create categories

In the Organize Bin, click the Tags tab.

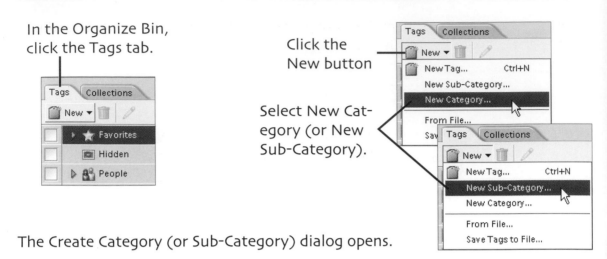

Click the New button

Select New Category (or New Sub-Category).

The Create Category (or Sub-Category) dialog opens.

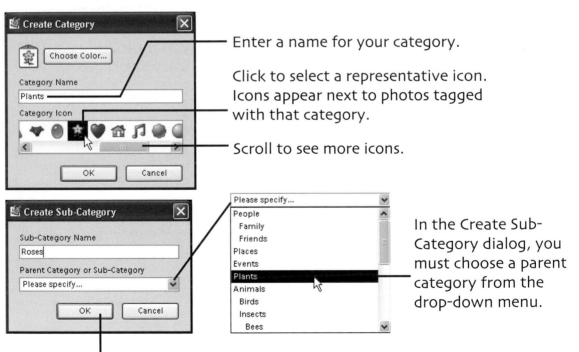

Enter a name for your category.

Click to select a representative icon. Icons appear next to photos tagged with that category.

Scroll to see more icons.

In the Create Sub-Category dialog, you must choose a parent category from the drop-down menu.

Click OK to close the dialog.

The new categories and sub-categories appear in the Organize Bin.

creating structure within your catalog

create tags

Creating tags is similar to creating categories and sub-catgories. Make tags the most specific level of your hierarchy.

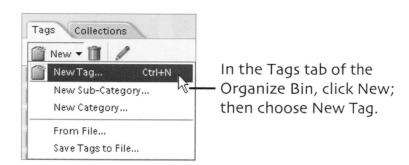

In the Tags tab of the Organize Bin, click New; then choose New Tag.

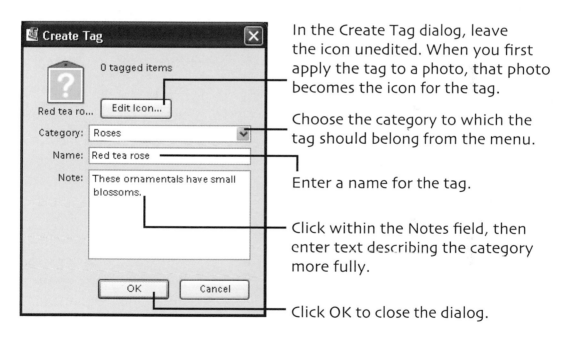

In the Create Tag dialog, leave the icon unedited. When you first apply the tag to a photo, that photo becomes the icon for the tag.

Choose the category to which the tag should belong from the menu.

Enter a name for the tag.

Click within the Notes field, then enter text describing the category more fully.

Click OK to close the dialog.

Tags appear below their parent category in the Organize Bin. Click a triangle to show/hide lower levels.

assign tags

Click a photo in the
Photo Browser to
select the photo.

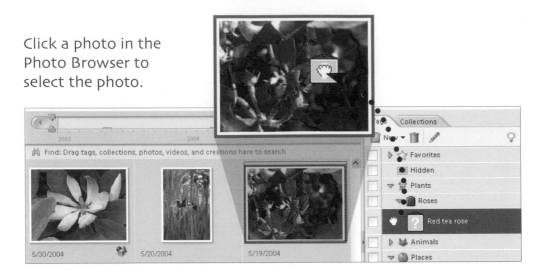

Drag the tag from the Organize Bin onto the selected image.

The icon for the
top-level category
appears beneath
the photo in the
Photo Browser.

A thumbnail of the first image
to which you apply the tag
becomes the tag icon in the
Organize Bin.

Drag a tag to one photo in a
group of selected photos to
apply the tag to all of them.
Use Shift-click to select a
range of contiguous photos;
Ctrl-click to select non-
contiguous photos.

creating structure within your catalog

add collections/groups

Elements' collection feature helps you gather and work with the photos you want to use in an album. When you sort photos by tags and categories, photos appear strictly in date order; in collections you can put images in any order.

1 In the Organize Bin, click the Collections tab.

2 Click New; then choose New Collection Group.

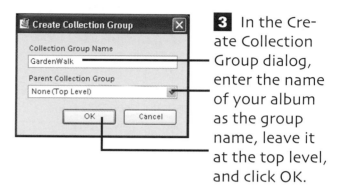

3 In the Create Collection Group dialog, enter the name of your album as the group name, leave it at the top level, and click OK.

4 Click New again; this time, choose New Collection.

5 In the Create Collection dialog, select your album as the Group, for Name enter TitlePage. Add notes if you like.

Click OK to close the dialog.

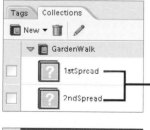

Repeat Steps 4 and 5 above to create collections for each spread (a set of facing pages). Our album needs a right-hand title page, nine spreads, and a left-hand last page.

It's useful to have a collection containing all the images you might use in your album. Name it AlbumCandidates. Collections appear in the Organize Bin.

creating structure within your catalog

search with tags

Once you have set up tags, use them to search for specific types of photos you'd like in your album. I think I'd like to use some bee photos in mine.

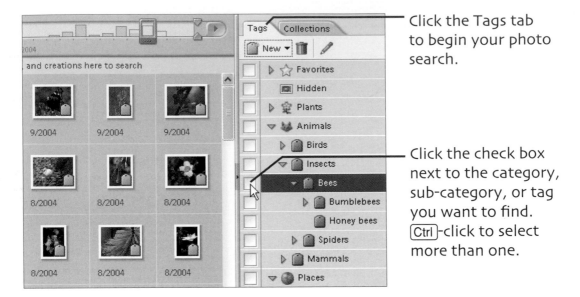

Click the Tags tab to begin your photo search.

Click the check box next to the category, sub-category, or tag you want to find. Ctrl-click to select more than one.

Check the Matching checkbox to display images that match your search criteria.

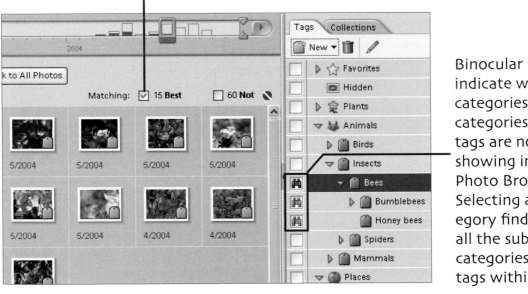

Binocular icons indicate which categories, sub-categories, and tags are now showing in the Photo Browser. Selecting a category finds all the sub-categories and tags within it.

creating structure within your catalog

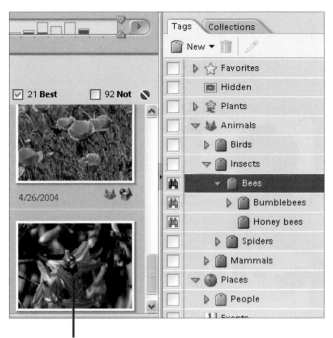

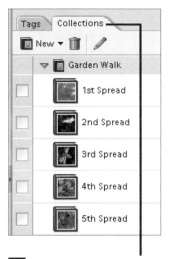

2 Click the Collections tab to view the collections you've prepared.

1 When you find an image that looks like a keeper for your album, click the photo to select it.

3 Drag the AlbumCandidates collection on top of the selected photo to add it to your collection of possible album photos.

creating structure within your catalog　　**21**

search with tags (cont.)

1 To assign multiple photos to a collection, click the first in a series of consecutive photos, then [Shift]-click the end of the range to select them all. Blue highlight shows that they're selected. To add more photos [Ctrl]-click them.

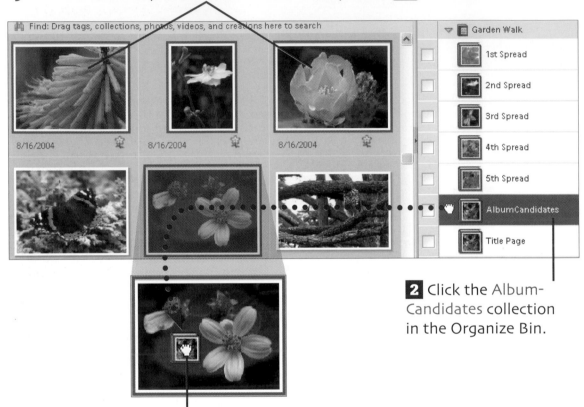

2 Click the Album-Candidates collection in the Organize Bin.

3 Drag the AlbumCandidates Collection onto one of the selected photos.

4 Organizer assigns the selected photos to that collection. The collection icon indicates that a photo belongs to one or more collections.

creating structure within your catalog

put photos in order

It's time to consider the sequence of photos in your album. First view your candidate photos by calling up the AlbumCandidates collection. Play with the order.

To review the photos you've gathered, in the Collections tab in the Organize Bin, click the check box for the AlbumCandidates collection.

The Photo Browser numbers the collection's contents, but the order is flexible. You can change it.

Click and drag a photo; the yellow bar previews the new location.

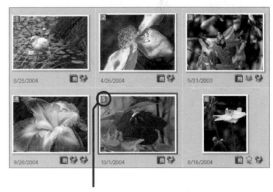

Release the mouse; the photo order and numbers update.

You can also drag multiple selected photos to a new location.

think in spreads

You've got the photos generally in order, now you need to break the order down into specific pages and spreads. Our album consists of a title page (a right-hand page), nine spreads (left- and right-hand pages), and a left-hand page at the end—20 pages in all. Assigning photos that belong together (on a page or on a spread) to a separate collection makes it easier to edit those photos to look good together (see Chapter 3).

Assign your title-page photo to the TitlePage collection you already created (see page 19); drag the TitlePage collection from the Organize Bin to the photo.

Select the photos that will go together on one spread. (Each page holds up to four photos, a possible total of eight photos per spread). Drag the appropriate Spread collection to one of the selected photos. Assign photos to each collection you created for the album.

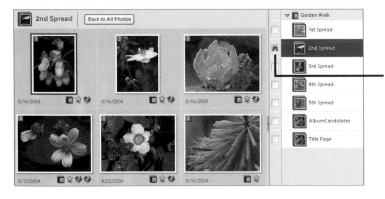

To view just the photos for one spread, click the check box for that collection.

extra bits

add captions & notes p. 14

- Click an icon at the top of the Properties window to view more data. The Tags view shows categories, tags, and collections to which the photo belongs. The History view shows the photo's place in a version set (see Chapter 3). The Metadata view shows data recorded by your digital camera, such as camera make and F-stop.

create categories p. 16

- In the Create Category dialog, clicking the Choose Color button opens a color picker. Choose the category tag's color; click OK.

- You can change the order of tags, categories, sub-categories, collections, and collection groups in the Organize Bin. In Organizer, choose Edit > Preferences > Tags and Collections. In the Enable Manual Sorting Option section, check the Manual radio button for Collections, for example. You can now drag collections listed in the bin to change their order.

create tags p. 17

- If you want to assign the image that appears in the tag icon right away, you must import it. Click the Edit Icon button in the Cre-

ate Tag dialog. The Edit Tag Icon dialog appears. Click the Import button; the Import Image for Tag Icon dialog appears. It's a file-import dialog that displays thumbnails of photo files. Navigate to the photo file you want to use as the icon image. Click the photo's thumbnail in the dialog, then click the Open button. The file-import dialog closes and the photo appears in the Edit Tag Icon dialog; click the OK button to close that dialog. Your selected photo now appears as the icon in the Create Tag dialog. Finish entering your tag name and notes; then click the OK button to close that dialog.

- You can edit a tag's name, notes, and/or icon at any time. Click the tag's name in the Organize Bin to select the tag. Then click the Edit Tag button at the top of the Organize Bin (the small pencil icon) to open the Edit Tag dialog.

- To change the size of icons in the Organize Bin, choose Edit > Preferences > Tags and Collections. Click the radio button for the size you like under Tag Display.

extra bits

add collections/ groups p. 19

- A tag or collection dropped onto an unselected photo applies to that photo only, even if other photos are selected. If you have multiple images selected and drop a tag on one of them, that tag applies to all the selected images.

- Creating collections and groups for each page or spread sounds like a lot of work. It's not absolutely necessary, but because you cannot safely edit images that are included in an album without jeopardizing the album, it's a good idea. These collections facilitate the process of editing images that appear together. If you're not used to working with photos on spreads, consider your first few albums warm ups for getting the hang of how photos can work together.

search with tags p. 20

- To exclude categories or tags from a search, right-click the check box and choose Exclude Photos with . . . from the menu.

3. fixing image flaws

You've made collections for all the pages in your album; but the photos that go on those pages may need some retouching. Elements Editor is your darkroom, providing the tools you need to make your photos look their best. Editor's two modes, Quick Fix and Standard Edit, offer different levels of edit functions, ranging from completely automated to fully user driven. In this project, we want to concentrate on learning to create album pages, not tweaking images to perfection. To fix image flaws quickly, we'll use a mix of automated tools and tools that give the user some control. You'll find most of these tools in Quick Fix mode. A few tools, such as the healing brush, are available only in Standard Edit mode, the mode that gives you the most control over photo retouching. For the sake of space, we'll mostly look at correcting one photo, with one problem, at a time. For your own album, be sure to look at all the photos for a spread together to evaluate what kinds of changes need to be made. If you keep all the images for the spread open simultaneously, you can harmonize them more easily.

enter Quick Fix mode

In Organizer, you're going to call up each collection you made in Chapter 2.

With the Collections tab foremost in the Organize Bin, click the check box for a collection.

The photos in that collection appear in the Photo Browser.

To select a photo for editing, click it.

Click the edit button and choose Go to Quick Fix from the drop-down menu.

Editor opens its own work area and displays the photo in Quick Fix mode.

Photos from some digital cameras include special printing data. If yours does, this warning appears. Check the Don't Show Again check box, and click OK. You can't edit a photo and keep this information. We'll save each edited photo in a new file; the original retains any special print data should you want to use it to print the photo later.

fixing image flaws

set preview parameters

In Quick Fix mode you have several different views for previewing your edits.

Choose the zoom tool to change magnification. Click the plus icon (+), then click the photo with the tool to zoom in; click the minus icon (-), then click the photo to zoom out.

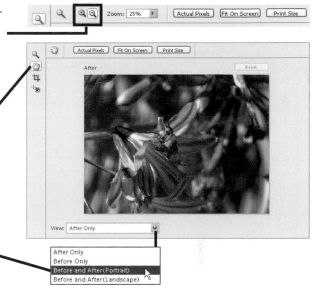

Use the hand tool to position the photo in the viewing area.

From the View menu choose Before and After (Portrait) to compare photos side by side.

With the zoom or hand tool selected, you can choose from three preset view sizes. Click a button to switch sizes.

Actual Pixels view (100%) is good for detail work.

Fit on Screen lets you see full photo context.

Print Size is a good compromise view.

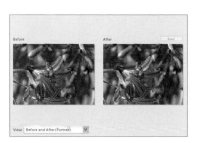

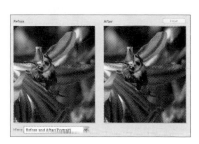

crop your photos

Most photos benefit from cropping (a fancy way to say trimming) to improve the subject's framing. For our project, crop photos to an aspect ratio of 3:4. The crop tool works similarly in both Editor modes. Try it in Quick Fix mode.

Click the crop tool button.

In the Options Bar, for width, enter 4 inches (for landscape orientation) or 3 (for portrait).

For height, enter 3 inches (for landscape orientation) or 4 (for portrait).

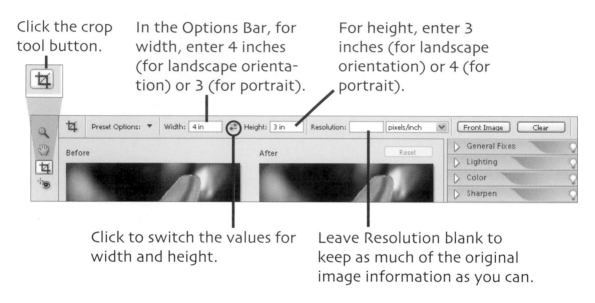

Click to switch the values for width and height.

Leave Resolution blank to keep as much of the original image information as you can.

Position the crop tool over the After photo. (The tool turns into the international No symbol over the Before image.)

Position the crop tool about where you want to begin the new image area.

Drag to create the crop; it need not be exact at first.

The rectangular marquee shows the proposed crop.

Darker, shielded, areas will get trimmed.

To fine-tune the crop, drag any of the four corner handles.

Position the pointer a bit away from a handle to activate the rotate pointer.

Drag to rotate the crop. Use this feature to straighten off-kilter photos.

Drag inside the marquee to move the whole crop rectangle.

Before and After views help you judge the crop.

Click Reset to start over at any time.

To cancel the crop, click the Cancel button.

To complete the crop, click the Commit button.

save your file

After you finish making edits to a file (in this case, cropping), choose File > Save to save the changes to your file.

Choose a location for the saved file. By default Elements puts the new version in the same location as the original you just worked from.

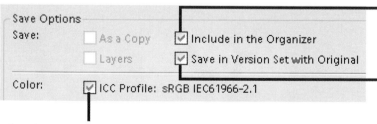

Click to view recently used folders or main locations.

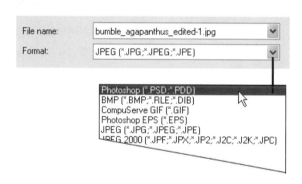

JPEG is a common photo format and will work fine in our album project (see the extra bits, page 52). If you prefer, you can select a new file format from the drop-down menu. We'll work with Photoshop (.psd) format files later in this chapter.

Choose Include in the Organizer and Save In Version Set with Original to preserve your original file. Editor saves changes in a copy, adding the word edited and a version number to the file name.

Check the ICC Profile check box to get the best color management for your album.

Click Save to
begin saving
your file.

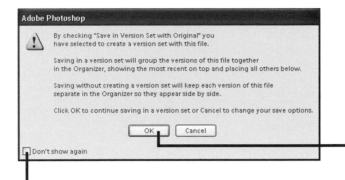

A warning
dialog appears
describing what
saving as a ver-
sion set entails.

Click OK to close
the dialog.

To avoid seeing this message for every photo you edit,
check the Don't Show Again check box.

When you save a JPEG file, the JPEG
Options dialog appears. Drag the quality slider all the way to the right or enter
12 in the Quality field. Maximum quality
and large file size produce the best results
in printed albums.

To close the file in Editor, click the Close
icon of the item being edited.

While a photo is
open in Editor,
its thumbnail
becomes locked
in Organizer's
Photo Browser.

After you close
the file in Editor,
the Photo Browser
thumbnail bears
a version set icon,
meaning this
thumbnail repre-
sents a group of
edited files.

fix red eyes

A flash positioned right above the camera lens (as in most point-and-shoot cameras) sends light straight out. If your subject is a face, the light enters the eye, hits the retina, and bounces straight back to the camera, picking up the retina's rich red color. The result: your friends look like angry alien creatures. We'll use the red-eye removal tool in Quick Fix mode; it's available in Standard Edit, too.

Dragging over a value name activates a double-arrow cursor. Drag left and right to change values. Release the mouse to enter the current value.

To open a slider, click the triangle to the right of a value field. Drag to change values. Click outside the slider to enter the current value.

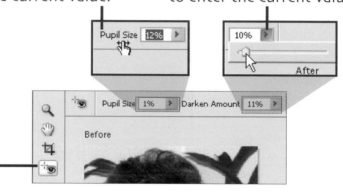

1 Click the cursor-and-eye icon to select the red-eye removal tool.

2 Enter a low value for Pupil Size; 12% is plenty.

Enter a low value for Darken Amount; 10% usually works well.

fixing image flaws

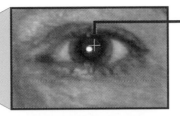

3 Position the pointer over any part of the red pupil in one of the eyes. Then click.

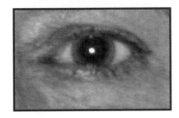

The red in the pupil area changes to black; other red areas retain their red color.

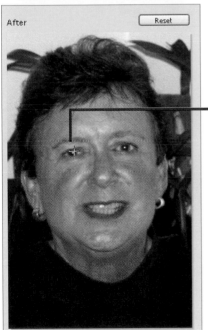

4 Repeat the procedure for the other eye.

The results are quite amazing. Your friends quickly regain their friendly appearance.

fixing image flaws

fix multiple flaws

The correction tools in the bin on the right side of the work area in Quick Fix mode let you correct photo flaws easily (though with less control and sophistication than you can achieve using the Standard Edit tools). The General Fixes section is a good starting place; the Smart Fix tool attempts to correct three problem areas at once: tonal range (exposure), color, and sharpness (focus).

Click the triangle to open General Fixes.

Click the Auto button to let Editor make its best guess at corrections.

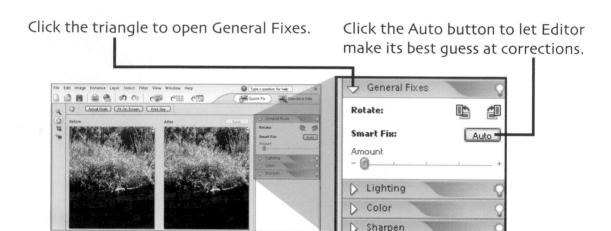

To undo the correction, click the Reset button.

Auto Smart Fix brings out details in the problem area without changing the rest of the photo.

The wall in shadow is underexposed.

fine-tune Smart Fix

Here Auto Smart Fix goes in the right direction but too far. The rose's leaves and petals look washed out. Fine-tune the correction with the Amount slider.

After trying an Auto correction, you must click the Reset button to return to your original photo before trying a new correction.

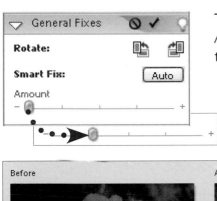

This time, drag the slider to apply Smart Fix. The After photo updates interactively. The farther to the right you drag, the stronger the correction.

Dragging to the first notch looks good.

To undo Amount slider changes, click the Cancel button.

To finalize slider changes, click the Commit button.

fix exposure flaws

Sometimes the Smart Fix correction is just not what you want at all. In this underexposed photo, Smart Fix's Auto correction makes the image too blue.

Click the Reset button to try another fix.

If Smart Fix spoils the color, try the Lighting corrections. Click the triangle to open the Lighting section.

Start with Levels. Click the Auto button.

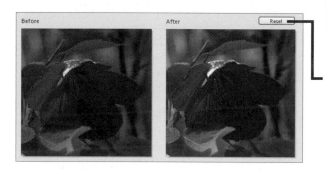

In this photo, Auto Levels does a little, but not enough. Click the Reset button to try another fix.

Try Contrast. Click the Auto button.

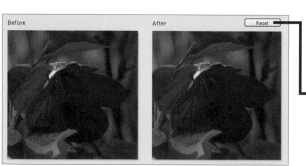

In this photo the Auto Contrast changes are even less helpful. Click the Reset button to try another fix.

fixing image flaws

It's time to try the interactive correction sliders. You can adjust different parts of your photo separately, judging visually what makes the best correction.

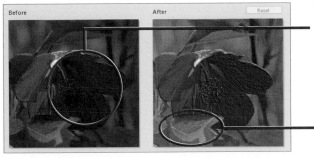

To bring out details where the shadow is too dark inside the flower, drag the Lighten Shadows slider to the right.

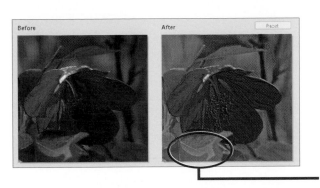

Now detail shows in the shadow, but the bright leaf areas are washed out. Drag the Darken Highlights slider to the right to bring them down.

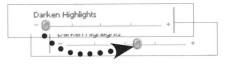

The leaves look a bit better.

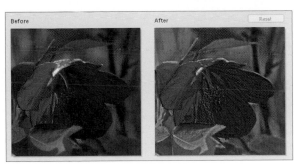

Finally, adjust the Midtone Contrast. Drag the slider to the right to increase contrast, to the left to decrease it. Here adding contrast brings back the leaves more.

With the Lighting sliders set, click the Commit button.

fixing image flaws

fix exposure flaws (cont.)

You can also use the corrections in the Lighting section to fix overexposed photos. For this photo, none of the automatic corrections (Auto Smart Fix, Auto Levels, or Auto Contrast) went far enough to correct the flat washed-out look.

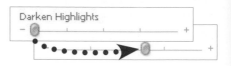

Drag the Darken Highlights slider to the right to create a darker image with more impact.

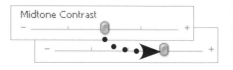

Drag the Midtone Contrast slider to the right to bring out more definition in the feathers and make the hawk stand out more.

With the Lighting sliders set, click the Commit button.

fixing image flaws

fix color cast

Photos taken under certain lighting conditions (such as on overcast days or indoors) may take on a color cast. Quick Fix's color-correction tools help you remove a color cast.

Click the triangle to access Quick Fix mode's color-correction tools.

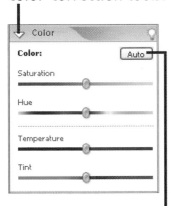

Auto Color did a bad job on this photo. Click the Reset button to start over.

Click the Auto button for Editor's best-guess correction.

Drag the Temperature slider to the right to warm up a photo with a blue color cast.

The result is better, but now it looks too green.

Drag the Tint slider to the right to reduce the green.

fix color cast (cont.)

As a final correction for this photo, dragging the Saturation slider to the left makes the color a bit less intense (a bit closer to black and white), giving the photo more of the mood of the weather the day it was taken, without the odd color cast.

When you've adjusted the photo to your satisfaction with the Color sliders, you must click the Commit button to apply the changes to your file.

If you find the color sliders confusing, try Editor's one-click trick for removing color cast. It's available in both Quick Fix and Standard Edit.

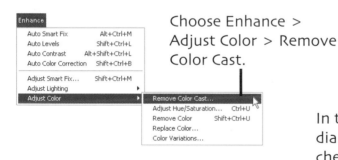

Choose Enhance > Adjust Color > Remove Color Cast.

In the Remove Color Cast dialog, check the Preview check box to see changes in the After view.

The pointer becomes an eye dropper. Use it to click an area of the photo that should be gray.

If you like the change click OK.

If not, click Reset and click another area. Try clicking an area that should be black or white.

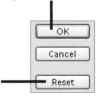

harmonize colors

When editing photos that appear together on a page or spread, it's good to open them together. That way you can make sure they look harmonious together.

To view multiple photos simultaneously, you must open them in Standard Edit mode.

1 In Organizer, click the Collections tab to access the collections you made earlier.

2 Choose the check box for a spread whose photos you want to work on.

3 Press Ctrl+A to select all photos.

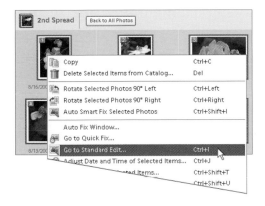

4 To open the photos in separate windows in Standard Edit mode, right-click a photo and choose Go to Standard Edit from the contextual menu.

5 Click the Tile Windows icon to see the photos simultaneously.

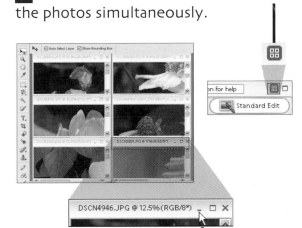

Click the Minimize icon to remove a photo from the work area but keep it available in the Photo Bin.

6 To reopen a photo double-click it in the Photo Bin.

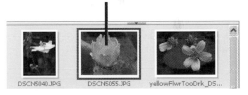

7 Drag any corner or edge of a window to resize the photo.

harmonize colors (cont)

Standard Edit mode allows you to work in layers. Using layers is beyond the scope of this book, but one basic layer trick is to make a duplicate layer of your photo before you start editing. If you don't like your edits, just delete the layer.

To copy your photo to a new layer, click the More triangle and choose Duplicate Layer from the Layers palette menu.

The duplicate layer appears in the Layers palette above the original.

Click the Trash icon to delete the active layer.

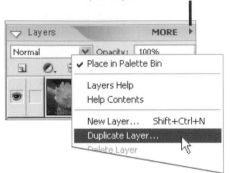

To hide a layer, click its eye icon.

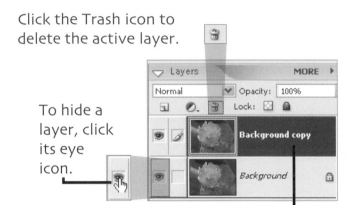

To choose the layer to work on (the active layer), in the Layers palette, click the layer; it highlights.

To start harmonizing colors, choose Enhance > Adjust Color > Color Variations.

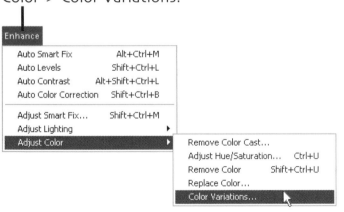

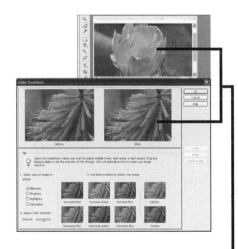

Position the Color Variations dialog so the After preview is near the photo you're trying to match.

The tubular blossoms should be less red to match the cactus flower. Click each radio button in turn to try changing different areas of the photo; view the thumbnails to see if any of them make changes in the direction you want. For this photo, changing the shadows does little; changing the midtones looks like the best bet.

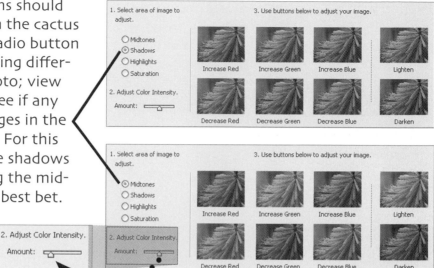

Dragging the Amount slider to the left lets you make the changes in subtle increments.

Click repeatedly to make the change more intense.

After one click.   After two clicks.

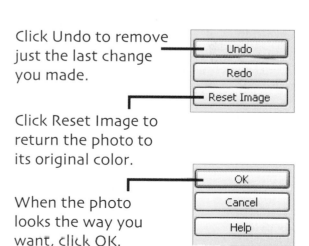

Click the thumbnail that makes the desired change, here Decrease Red fits best.

Decrease Red

Click Undo to remove just the last change you made.

Undo

Redo

Reset Image

Click Reset Image to return the photo to its original color.

When the photo looks the way you want, click OK.

OK

Cancel

Help

fixing image flaws

clean up photos

Even in a lovely spot like the arboretum, trash can spoil a nice shot. Elements' healing brush tool makes it easy to clean up after litter bugs. The healing brush is unavailable in Quick Fix mode. You must open your photo in Standard Edit.

To work on a copy of the image, drag the Background layer to the Create New Layer icon.

Select the zoom tool. You'll want to get a close up view of the area you want to clean up.

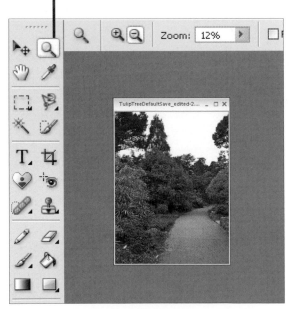

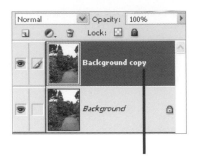

Click the Background copy layer to activate it.

Position the zoom tool in the area you want to clean.

Drag a rectangle around the area.

In the tool box, select the healing brush (or spot healing brush) tool.

The spot healing brush works well on small items.

Click the triangle to open the preset brush menu.

Drag to choose brush size.

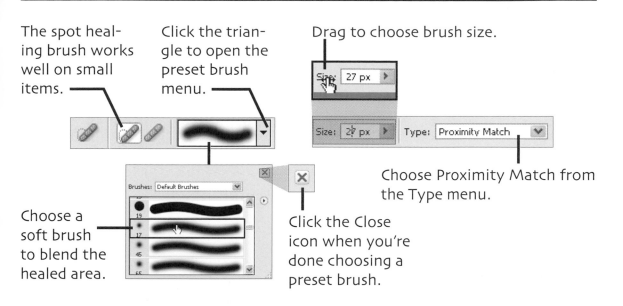

Choose a soft brush to blend the healed area.

Click the Close icon when you're done choosing a preset brush.

Choose Proximity Match from the Type menu.

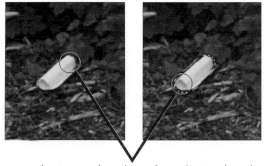

Unwanted items surrounded by uniform objects, like these dried sticks, heal pretty seamlessly. It may take a few tries to get it just right.

Use the spot healing brush (or healing brush) tool to "paint" over an unwanted item in your photo. Here it's trash lying near the path.

Release the mouse button and the healing takes place.

If some traces of the object remain, paint over them again to make them blend in completely.

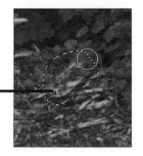

fixing image flaws

sharpen in Quick Fix

The final correction to talk about is sharpening—and I do mean final. Sharpen your photo after you've made all other corrections. Sharpening makes the edges of things more distinct and brings out detail. Digital photo prints are often a bit softer than photos printed from film. Sharpening helps bring out that extra touch of focus. But use sharpening sparingly. It's easy to get carried away and sharpen too much, especially using Editor's automated sharpening tools.

Open your photo in Quick Fix mode.

Click the triangle to open the Sharpen section.

Click to select the hand tool. The tool lets you reposition your photo preview to check how various areas look with the sharpening that you add.

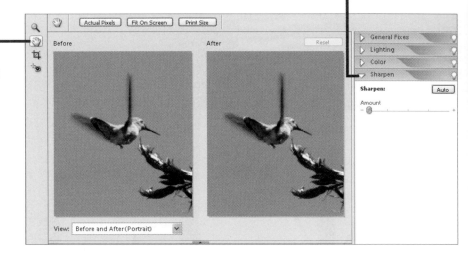

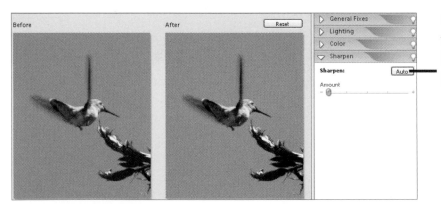

Click the Auto button to apply Editor's best-guess sharpening to your photo.

fixing image flaws

It's important to check the results of sharpening by viewing your photo at 100 percent. This view reveals if oversharpening is happening. Oversharpening creates extra noise and artifacts in your image.

Click the Actual Pixels button to view your photo at 100%.

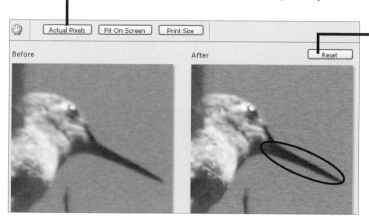

Click the Reset button to try a different correction.

Auto Sharpen frequently takes the correction too far. In this photo, artifacts appear along the top edge of the beak after choosing Auto Sharpen.

Clicking the slider half way to the first notch applies good sharpening for this photo.

Move the slider to the right to apply more sharpening. By the second notch, artifacts already appear. Move the slider any farther right and you start getting a halo effect.

To undo your adjustments, click Cancel. To accept your adjustments, click Commit.

fixing image flaws

prune your collections

We've been saving each edited photo in a version set with its original. Generally, the Photo Browser stacks a new version on top of its original. When displaying a collection, however, the browser doesn't show version sets. The original photos you assigned to the collection and any edited versions of those photos appear as separate files. Having multiple copies of the photos adds confusion when it's time to place your photos in their album (which we'll do in Chapters 4 and 5). Return to the Photo Browser to prune your collections of outdated photos.

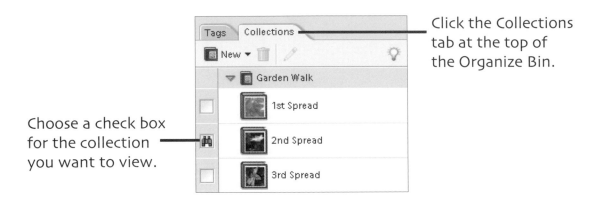

Click the Collections tab at the top of the Organize Bin.

Choose a check box for the collection you want to view.

Originals of any edited photos appear at the beginning of the collection.

Edited photos (and originals of unedited photos) follow the outdated originals and appear in the order that you chose for the collection.

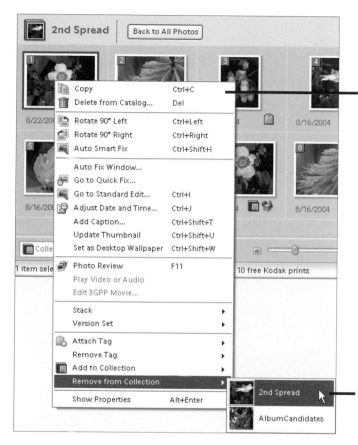

To begin the pruning process, right-click a photo that you wan to remove. The contextual menu opens.

Choose Remove from Collection. From the fly-out menu, choose 2nd Spread (or whichever Spread collection the photo belongs to).

When you've done this for each outdated photo in the collection, the Photo Browser displays just the versions of the photos that you will use in your album.

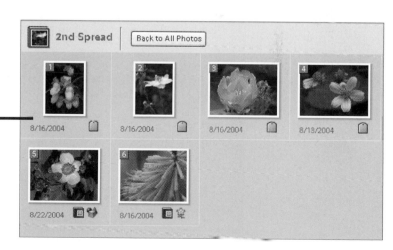

fixing image flaws

extra bits

crop your photos p. 30

- Most of the Elements albums have built-in borders that frame your photos. The aspect ratio (ratio of width to height) for album borders is 4:3 (landscape) or 3:4 (portrait). This is a common ratio for digital cameras. If a photo has a different ratio, however, Elements' Album Creation wizard simply crops the photo. To keep control over what part of your photo appears in your album, crop photos to 3:4 yourself.

- The No Borders style (for printing album pages on your own printer), accepts photos with any aspect ratio. You might expect that to be the case with No Borders Book and Full Bleed Book styles too, but as this Visual QuickProject went to press, that wasn't true. Photos in those styles get cropped to the 3:4 ratio. Adobe plans to update templates and give you more control over aspect ratio in these styles in the future (see Chapters 4 and 5).

- By default, the cropping shield is black with 75 percent opacity. After you draw a cropping rectangle, you can choose a new color and opacity in the Options bar.

save your file p. 32

- Although JPEG is not usually a suitable format for printed books, Elements translates photo album pages to PDF format for printing (see Chapter 5). Therefore, you don't need to change file formats when you save your edited photos. It's fine to change JPEG (.jpg) files to Photoshop (.psd) files if you prefer. If you edit a photo in Standard Edit mode and add layers, Elements automatically changes the file's format to .psd for you.

- If you have access to an Epson printer that you might want to use for printing your photos, you can restore the P.I.M. warning when you're done with your album project. That way, the warning dialog pops up when you edit a photo that contains embedded Print Image Matching (P.I.M.) data. To restore the warning (and any others you've turned off), from the Organizer work area, choose Edit > Preferences > Editor Preferences. In the Preferences dialog that appears, click the Reset All Warning Dialogs button. If you are already working in the Editor work area, choose Edit > Preferences > General to open the dialog.

fixing image flaws

fix red eyes p. 34

- For Pupil Size, enter no more than 50 % unless your want you subject to look as if he or she's just been to the eye doctor.

- For Darken Amount, 100 % would look unnaturally dark.

- Though the red-eye removal tool is a cross-hair cursor, and it lets you draw a selection rectangle, the tool works best if you just click once within a red pupil area. Only if that one click doesn't work should you try making a selection with the tool.

fix multiple flaws p. 36

- It's important to apply only one Auto correction from the Quick Fix tools. Try one, then if it's not what you want, click the Reset button and try something else. Applying more than one Auto correction quickly degrades the quality of your photo.

fine-tune Smart Fix p. 37

- The set of correction tools on the right side of the Quick Fix work area is divided into four sections. It's best to work in one section at a time; try a correction, then click the Cancel button if you want to try something else within the same section. Click the Commit button (or the Cancel button, if you decide not to make any change in that section) before moving on. If you've made slider adjustments in one section and then start adjusting sliders in a different section, Elements automatically commits the changes you made in the first section. The result may not be what you intended, in which case, you'll have to reset the photo and start all over again.

sharpen in Quick Fix p. 48

- Sharpening is truly an art. The amount of sharpening to apply depends on the type of photo, the subject matter and original intent for focus, as well as the final delivery medium. The amount of sharpening you need for images on the Web is different from the amount of sharpening you need for printed photos. Sharpening for a small photo in an album is different from sharpening for a large poster-sized print. If you want to move beyond the automated sharpening in Quick Fix mode, you'll need to use filters. You can access filters in both Quick Fix and Standard Edit mode. Choose

extra bits

sharpen in Quick Fix (cont.)

Filter > Sharpen to see a full list of sharpening filter choices. The Unsharp Mask filter is the standard professional sharpening tool. Experiment with its settings and your photos. But remember, it may take some time (or some expert advice from the many excellent books on Photoshop Elements of Photoshop) to learn how to get the best results using the sharpening filters.

4. creating albums with fixed layouts

Photoshop Elements 3.0 comes with an Album Creation wizard and templates for creating photo album pages in various styles. Some styles place photos inside a border, others are borderless. Borders can provide decorative frames, add drop shadows, or give digital photos the white edges of traditional prints. Styles with borders have fixed layouts. Borderless styles place photos in a default layout, but without frames, leaving you free to reposition the photos

The basics of working with photos and text in albums are the same with or without borders. The easiest styles to use have borders and a fixed layout. For your first project, try a fixed-border layout in a style designed to be printed on 8.5-by-11-inch paper on your home printer (these styles lack the yellow Order Online medallion). Once you've created a basic album, you'll be ready to tackle something more creative in Chapter 5.

The templates that shipped with Elements 3.0 use borders with an aspect ratio of 3:4 (or 4:3). The wizard crops photos that have any other aspect ratio to fit. To get the best framing for your photos, crop them to the 3:4 ratio yourself (see Chapter 3).

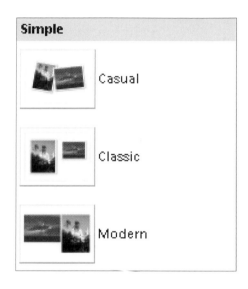

get new templates

Before working with the Album Creation wizard, update the templates.

1 To start the update process, open Organizer; choose Edit > Preferences > Services.

Adobe may use updates to correct template problems discovered since Elements shipped. Adobe will also use updates to add new styles.

2 Select Services in the Preferences dialog.

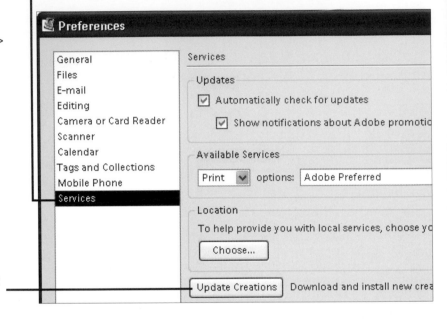

3 Click Update Creations.

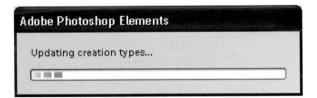

4 Elements connects to the Internet and downloads any new templates.

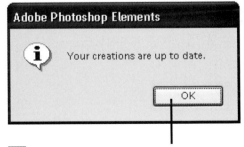

5 Click OK to finish updating.

6 Click OK to close the Preferences dialog.

creating albums with fixed layouts

open creations wizard

In Organizer, click the Create button in the shortcuts bar.

The Creation Setup wizard opens. It offers seven types of creative projects that you can make with your photos.

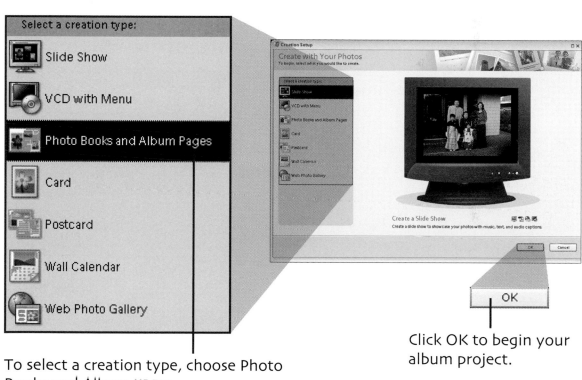

To select a creation type, choose Photo Books and Album Pages.

Click OK to begin your album project.

choose album style

 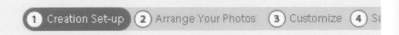
The Album Creation wizard opens. In Step 1: Creation Set-up, you set parameters. For your first album, choose a style with borders that you can print on a home printer. For now, avoid the borderless styles (grouped under the heading Full Photo) and the styles designed to be ordered as books (the ones that include the word Book in their name and have yellow medallions that say Order Online).

Casual is a nice clean-looking style that's not too formal. Click the name to select it for this first album project.

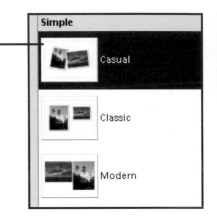

Check all of the Options. You can customize any item, except page numbers, as you lay out your album pages. Page numbers are the only items you can't change. You should know that for hardcover books, the page numbers are strange. Odd-numbers show up on left-hand pages, evens on the right. In professionally designed books, it's exactly the opposite. For home-printed, single-sided pages, however, the default page numbers look fine.

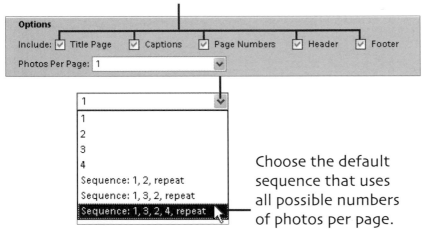

Choose the default sequence that uses all possible numbers of photos per page.

When you finish choosing album parameters, click Next Step.

choose photos

In Step 2: Arrange Your Photos, you bring photos into your album.

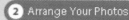

Click the Add photos
button to start.

The radio buttons
and check boxes
in the Add Photos
From section filter
the images in your
catalog. By default,
this dialog displays
the photos cur-
rently selected in
Organizer's Photo
Browser.

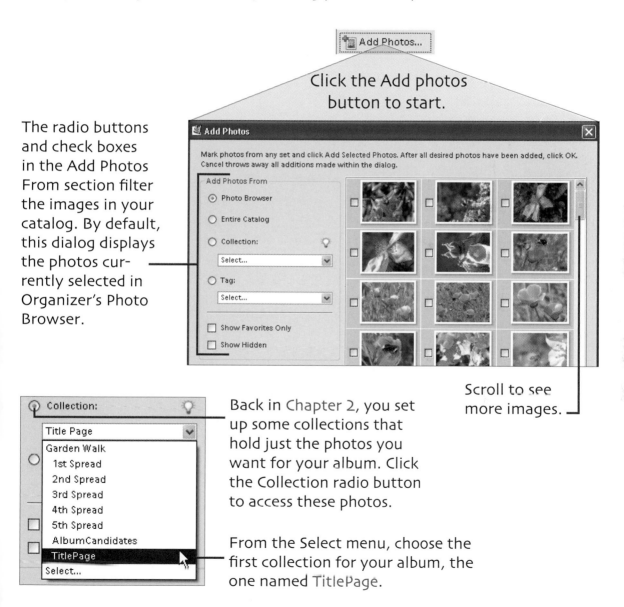

Scroll to see
more images.

Back in Chapter 2, you set
up some collections that
hold just the photos you
want for your album. Click
the Collection radio button
to access these photos.

From the Select menu, choose the
first collection for your album, the
one named TitlePage.

choose photos (cont.)

Click the check box to select your Title-page image.

Click Add Selected Photos to bring the checked images into your album.

Next, select the collection named 1stSpread to bring those photos into the Add Photos dialog.

Click the check boxes to select the photos.

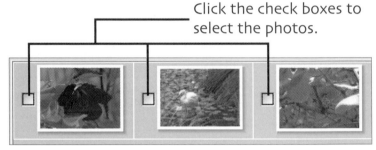

Repeat this selection process for the rest of the collections you set up.

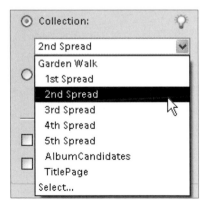

When you've added all your photos, click OK to close the Add Photos dialog.

creating albums with fixed layouts

put photos in order

You can change the order of your images in Step 2: Arrange Your Photos.

1 Click the photo you want to move, then drag it to a new position. (To move several photos, Ctrl-click each one; if the photos are in a row, click the first one, then Shift-click the last one to select them all. Dragging one photo moves the whole selected group, even if the photos are not contiguous.)

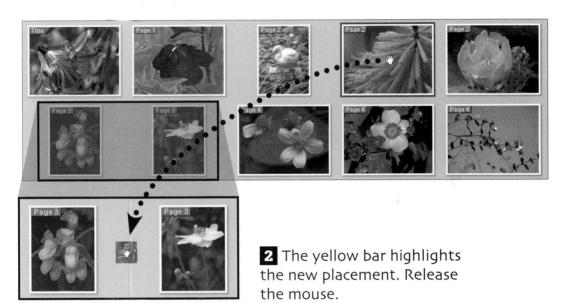

2 The yellow bar highlights the new placement. Release the mouse.

3 The Album Creation wizard reorders the images and reassigns their pages.

put photos in order (cont.)

In Step 2: Arrange Your Photos, the Album Creation wizard lets you reuse photos without duplicating files. You can also remove photos from an Album here.

Let's repeat the Title photo on Page 1. (We're making a home-printed album, but for hardcover books, the wizard crops the Title photo to fit the die-cut square in the album cover. You might want to show off the full image as your first page.) Click the Title photo to select it.

Then click the Use Photo Again button.

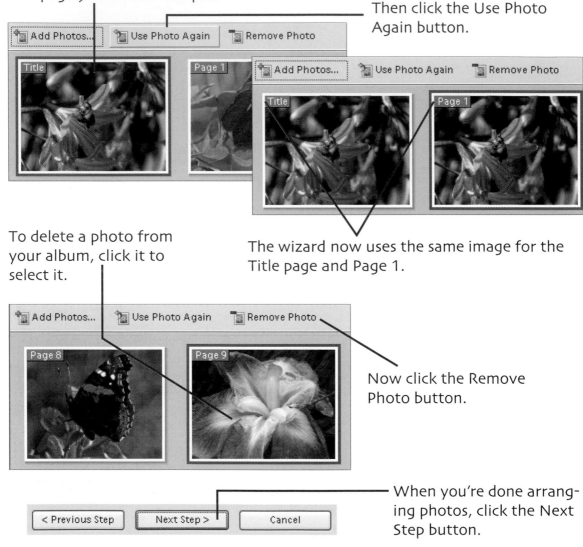

The wizard now uses the same image for the Title page and Page 1.

To delete a photo from your album, click it to select it.

Now click the Remove Photo button.

When you're done arranging photos, click the Next Step button.

creating albums with fixed layouts

fine-tune the layout

Step 3: Customize   Creation Set-up ② Arrange Your Photos ③ Customize ④ Save

In Step 3: Customize, you fine-tune the layout. Album styles with borders aren't fully customizable, but you can enlarge what's in the frame and add text.

Page layouts vary according to album style, the number of photos per page, and the orientation of the images. The wizard places photos for you.

Before customizing, "flip" through your album to see how your layouts look.

To add, delete, or rearrange photos, click the Previous Step button to return to Step 2.

Click the Back button to move to the album's previous page.

Click the Forward button to move to the next album page.

< Previous Step

position photos

In a style with borders, the border always stays the same size, in the same spot on the page, and with the same aspect ratio (3:4). You can resize the image, to zoom in, then reposition the photo to determine what appears inside the frame.

Click a photo to select it and activate its selection rectangle. Place the pointer over a corner resize handle.

Drag the handle outward.

Release the handle to preview the image size; the dim area gets cropped. Drag the photo to move it.

Click outside the photo to deselect it and view the new cropping and enlargement.

creating albums with fixed layouts

add title text

1 Once you have all of the photos in place and sized as you want, you are ready to deal with the text elements of your layout. To return to the Title page, choose Title from the View Page menu.

2 A placeholder title appears automatically on the Title page. Click the title to activate its text box. Double-click the title to open a dialog for editing the title.

Double-Click to Insert Title

3 Drag, triple-click, or press [Ctrl]-[A] to select all the text in the Title dialog.

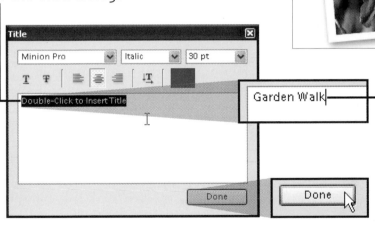

4 Enter new text for the title.

Garden Walk

5 Click the Done button to close the dialog.

6 The new title appears in the default font, style, size, and color. You'll learn to change these characteristics in Chapter 5.

Garden Walk

7 Click to go to Page 1.

edit headers & footers

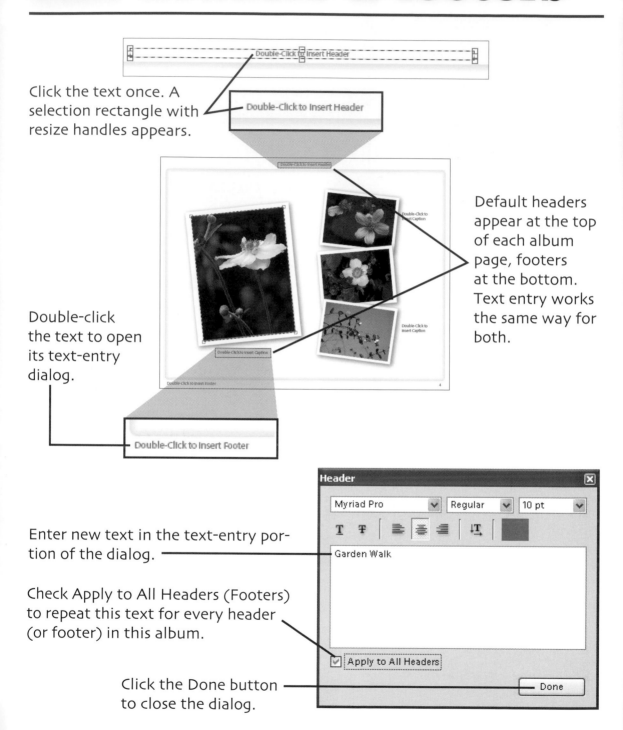

Click the text once. A selection rectangle with resize handles appears.

Double-Click to Insert Header

Default headers appear at the top of each album page, footers at the bottom. Text entry works the same way for both.

Double-click the text to open its text-entry dialog.

Double-Click to Insert Footer

Enter new text in the text-entry portion of the dialog.

Check Apply to All Headers (Footers) to repeat this text for every header (or footer) in this album.

Click the Done button to close the dialog.

Header

Myriad Pro | Regular | 10 pt

Garden Walk

☑ Apply to All Headers

Done

edit captions

Photos without captions in Organizer get placeholder captions in your album.

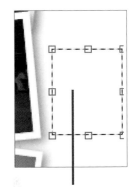

A "missing" caption, usually means you once clicked that photo's caption in Organizer, but entered no text.

In Step 3 of the wizard, click in the area of any "missing" caption to activate its selection rectangle.

Photos that have captions in Organizer bring their captions with them when you import them into an album.

Double-click any caption to open its text-entry dialog.

check resolution

The Album Creation wizard warns you when you try to include photos whose resolution is too low in your album. Importing low-resolution images results in a warning in Step 2: Arrange Your Photos.

You can resize even a high-resolution image so much that you put it beyond the limits of best print quality. This 300-ppi photo has plenty of resolution at this album's default single-photo size, but going wild with enlarging will put it beyond the limits.

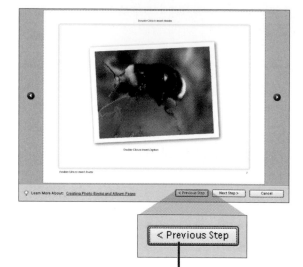

1 To see if your images have enough resolution after you have resized them in the album layout, click the Previous Step button to return to Step 2.

2 If you've enlarged a photo so that there's no longer enough resolution for best print quality, a warning dialog pops up every time you enter Step 2.

3 A warning triangle indicates problem photos. To insure best quality, go to Step 3 and reduce or reset the problem image (see extra bits page 71).

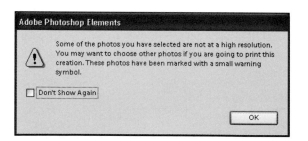

save and print

When you've finished positioning your photos and entering the text for headers, footers, and captions, it's time to save and print your album.

In Step 3, click the Next Step button to move to Step 4. (If starting from an earlier step, keep clicking Next Step until you reach Step 4.)

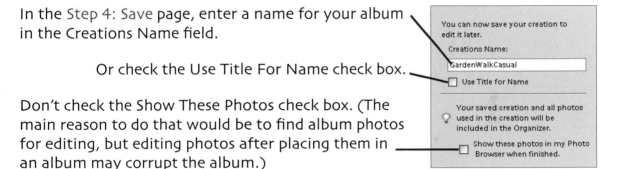

Step 4: Save ① Creation Set-up ② Arrange Your Photos ③ Customize ④ Save ⑤ Share

In the Step 4: Save page, enter a name for your album in the Creations Name field.

Or check the Use Title For Name check box.

Don't check the Show These Photos check box. (The main reason to do that would be to find album photos for editing, but editing photos after placing them in an album may corrupt the album.)

You can now save your creation to edit it later.

Creations Name:

GardenWalkCasual

☐ Use Title for Name

Your saved creation and all photos used in the creation will be included in the Organizer.

☐ Show these photos in my Photo Browser when finished.

Click the Save button to begin the process of saving your album. The wizard takes you automatically to Step 5.

< Previous Step   Save >

Step 5: Share ① Creation Set-up ② Arrange Your Photos ③ Customize ④ Save ⑤ Share

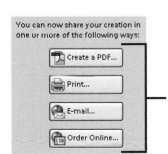

You can now share your creation in one or more of the following ways:

- Create a PDF...
- Print...
- E-mail...
- Order Online...

Step 5: Share offers options for printing and sharing your album. Skip these for now.

Click the Done button immediately (see extra bits, page 72, to learn why).

< Previous Step   Done

save and print (cont.)

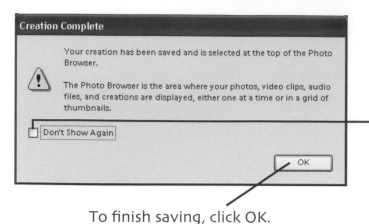

Creation Complete

Your creation has been saved and is selected at the top of the Photo Browser.

The Photo Browser is the area where your photos, video clips, audio files, and creations are displayed, either one at a time or in a grid of thumbnails.

Don't Show Again

OK

Saved albums become part of the current catalog in Organizer. Check the check box to avoid seeing this message for each album you save.

To finish saving, click OK.

Creation thumbnails bear a special icon.

A newly saved creation appears as the first item in Organizer's Photo Browser. Double-click the creation thumbnail to reopen the album in the Creation wizard.

When you open a saved album the Album Creation wizard takes you to Step 3. Click the Next Step button to move to Step 4.

Next Step >

To move on to Step 5, where you can print, click the Save button.

Save >

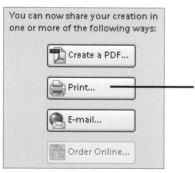

You can now share your creation in one or more of the following ways:

Create a PDF...

Print...

E-mail...

Order Online...

Click the Print button to print a test run on cheap paper or a final version on nice paper.

The dimensions of the album pages created by the Casual template measure 11 by 8.5 inches. In the settings for your printer, choose Landscape orientation for the paper. Choose a low print quality for test runs, high print quality for final prints.

creating albums with fixed layouts

extra bits

get new templates p. 56

- To update templates in Editor, choose Edit > Preferences > General. In the Services part of the Preferences dialog, check Automatically Check for Updates.

- Currently only one template style—No Borders—accepts photos in anything but the 3:4 (4:3) aspect ratio. The No Borders style must be printed on a local printer, not ordered as a photobook. Why might you want to work with other aspect ratios? Cropping to another aspect ratio may better frame a subject. A square crop, for example, might frame a face. Panoramic photos are a popular use of non-standard aspect ratios.

- Adobe plans to add templates that use aspect ratios other than 3:4 or 4:3. Be sure to keep checking for template updates.

choose photos p. 59

- Once you've brought photos into an album it's a good idea to save that work. Click the close icon for the Creation wizard; a dialog warns that the creation hasn't been saved. Go through all the save procedures outlined on pages 69 and 70. Just be sure to click the Done button to complete the save procedure. Then reopen your creation to continue editing it.

- Press Ctrl-A to check all the check boxes in the Add Photos dialog.

- Click in the gray area to uncheck any selected check boxes, or press Shift-Ctrl-A

fine-tune the layout p. 63

- If you set up your creation with a default series (for example, alternating pages of 1 and 2 photos), you can specify a new number of photos on a page by choosing the number from the Photos on This Page menu in Step 3. We'll do that in Chapter 5.

position photos p. 64

- If you don't like the resizing that you've done, click the Reset Photos button above the work area in Step 3 to return all photos on the page to their original size and position within their borders.

- When you resize within borders, dragging inward shrinks the image and leaves a wider border, which may look odd.

- Another way to deselect a photo or piece of text is to right-click it and choose deselect from the contextual menu.

extra bits

edit headers & footers p. 66

- Usually, it makes sense to click the Apply to All check box in the Header or Footer dialog on Page 1, even if you plan to change some on later pages. You can change individual headers or footers by double-clicking them and entering new text in the dialog.

- Be careful about clicking that box at later stages. The new header or footer overrides any previous header or footer text you entered.

edit captions p. 67

- What you type in an album caption has no effect on that photo's caption in Organizer.

- Don't make text changes until you've put your photos in order, chosen which pages they go on, and made any sizing changes. If you move a photo to a different page, you'll lose any caption text you've entered in the album.

- An advantage to creating captions in Organizer: they will be tied to the image and move with it.

save and print p. 69

- Resist the temptation to start sharing, printing, or making a PDF file until you've clicked the Done button. If you get caught up

in printing, for example, and close the wizard window before clicking the Done button, your album changes will not be saved.

- Many companies make glossy photo paper in 8.5-by-11-inch sheets suitable for use with your home color printer. Some sheets can even be printed on both sides. You can use a three-hole punch and place these sheets in notebooks or other types of binders. For starters, check out the following companies who list glossy photo paper in their product sections (usually under supplies and accessories): Canon (www.canon.com), Epson (www.epson.com), HP (www.hp.com), Kodak (www.kodak.com), and Strathmore (www.strathmoreartist.com). It's often possible to purchase glossy photo paper at discount office supply stores.

- In addition to paper that resembles photo prints, Strathmore makes 8.5-by-11-inch art papers, with various textures, that can be used on ink-jet printers and might dress up your album.

creating albums with fixed layouts

5. creating albums with flexible layouts

In the previous chapter you created an album in a simple fixed-layout style. To get more flexibility and exercise your creativity fully, you need to choose one of the Full Photo styles. When you choose one of these styles, the Album Creation wizard places your photos on the album pages without any borders. You can truly resize your photos (there's no frame to crop the enlarged image) and reposition photos on the album page.

One borderless style—No Borders—is designed for creating album pages that you can print on your home printer. At the time this book was being written, No Borders is the only style that allows you to work with photos that have an aspect ratio other than 3:4. For the future, Adobe plans to update templates to give you this freedom in the styles that create hardcover photobooks as well. For this project, we'll work with a style that gives you lots of creative license and that makes albums that can be printed as hardcover photobooks. (For more about updating templates and ordering photobooks, see Chapter 6.)

choose a flexible album

Open the Album Creation wizard, as described in Chapter 4.

Step 1: Creation Set-up

This time, in Step 1, choose No Borders Book as the album style.

Check all of the options for title page and text elements. The wizard still sets page numbers oddly in this style, but the numbers on each page help you to position photos and text correctly. You can delete them before ordering the photobook.

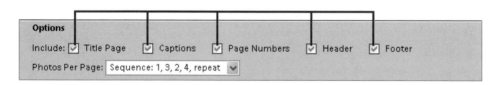

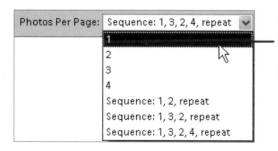

Choose 1 photo per page. It's easier to create a variety of multiple-image pages when no repeating series has been set up in advance.

Click Next Step.

Step 2: Arrange Your Photos

In Step 2, use the collections you've set up for your album to bring photos into the Album Creation wizard as described in Chapter 4.

creating albums with flexible layouts

customize title text

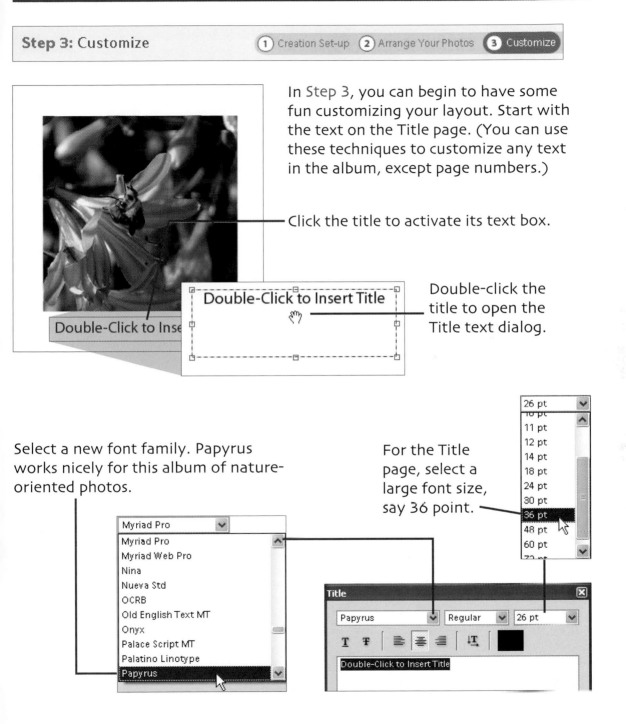

In Step 3, you can begin to have some fun customizing your layout. Start with the text on the Title page. (You can use these techniques to customize any text in the album, except page numbers.)

Click the title to activate its text box.

Double-Click to Insert Title

Double-click the title to open the Title text dialog.

Select a new font family. Papyrus works nicely for this album of nature-oriented photos.

For the Title page, select a large font size, say 36 point.

26 pt	
10 pt	
11 pt	
12 pt	
14 pt	
18 pt	
24 pt	
30 pt	
36 pt	
48 pt	
60 pt	

Myriad Pro
Myriad Pro
Myriad Web Pro
Nina
Nueva Std
OCRB
Old English Text MT
Onyx
Palace Script MT
Palatino Linotype
Papyrus

Title

Papyrus   Regular   26 pt

Double-Click to Insert Title

customize title text

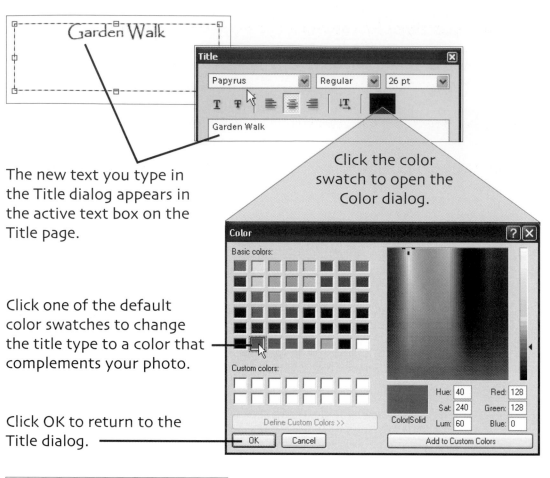

The new text you type in the Title dialog appears in the active text box on the Title page.

Click the color swatch to open the Color dialog.

Click one of the default color swatches to change the title type to a color that complements your photo.

Click OK to return to the Title dialog.

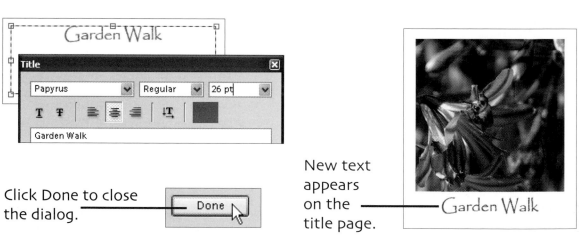

Click Done to close the dialog.

New text appears on the title page.

creating albums with flexible layouts

know the print area

The Full Photo album styles let you resize and reposition everything but the page number, but items that sit close to the edge of the page may disappear. A "page" in the Album Creation wizard measures 10.5 by 9 inches: the same dimensions as a photobook cover. Ofoto (the company that prints photobooks) trims the pages to fit inside the cover. The wizard doesn't explicitly define a safe area for photos and text, but you can visualize one yourself.

Imagine a rectangle bounded by the default header, footer, and page number. These items are sure to print; use them as guide to the safe-printing zone.

I've added orange highlighting to show the possible danger zone, but the wizard does not do that. You can't predict the final trim area precisely. Anything placed beyond the range of the default text elements runs the risk of getting chopped.

creating albums with flexible layouts

increase header size

Header text first appears on Page 1. In the No Borders Book style the default type is too small for my aging eyes. Let's choose something larger.

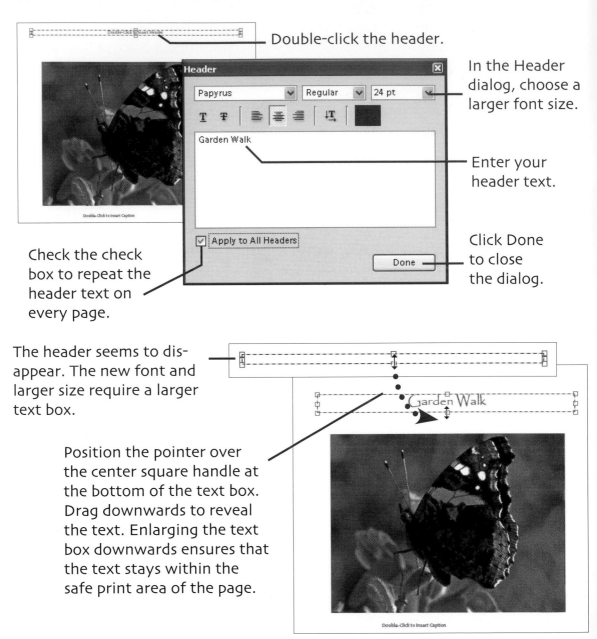

Double-click the header.

In the Header dialog, choose a larger font size.

Enter your header text.

Check the check box to repeat the header text on every page.

Click Done to close the dialog.

The header seems to disappear. The new font and larger size require a larger text box.

Position the pointer over the center square handle at the bottom of the text box. Drag downwards to reveal the text. Enlarging the text box downwards ensures that the text stays within the safe print area of the page.

increase footer size

1 Footers work the same way as headers. Double-click the footer to activate the text box and open the Footer dialog.

2 Choose your font and a size. For Papyrus, 14-point is easy to read but not overwhelming.

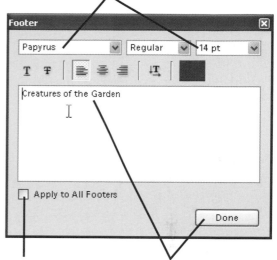

We'll use different footers on each page. Leave this box unchecked.

Enter footer text and click the Done button.

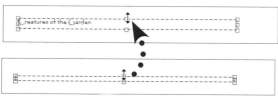

3 The new font is too big for the default text box. Drag the center handle upward to reveal the text. Drag upward to ensure that the footer stays in the safe-print zone.

4 Click any blank area of the page to deselect the text box. Now you can see the text without distraction.

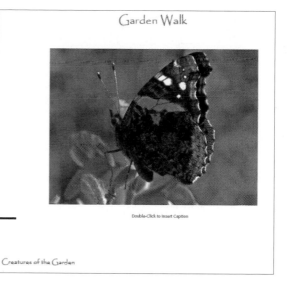

adjust captions

Double-click the caption to activate its text box and open the Caption dialog.

Choose the font and size. Use one font family for headers, footers, and captions for a clean professional look.

Single-photo pages look nice with the caption centered against the photo. Click the center-text option.

Enter caption text. (If the photo has a caption in Organizer, that caption appears here. You can leave it alone, or modify it just for the album.)

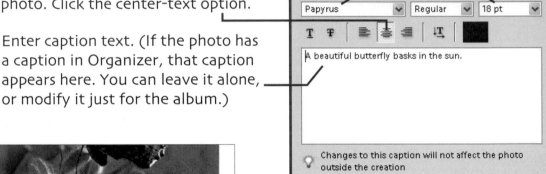

Caption

| Papyrus | Regular | 18 pt |

A beautiful butterfly basks in the sun.

Changes to this caption will not affect the photo outside the creation

Done

Click Done to close the dialog.

Drag the side handles of the text box to the right and to the left, aligning the box with the photo's edges. The text centers itself inside the text box.

Click any blank area of the page to deselect the text box.

Garden Walk

A beautiful butterfly basks in the sun.

lay out one photo

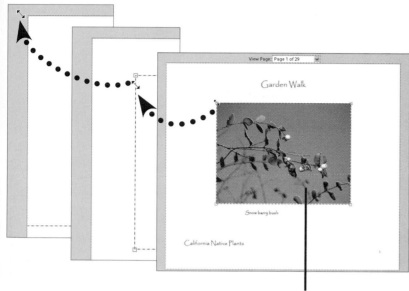

Single-photo pages look nice; the image is a good size. Still, you can increase the impact of some images by enlarging them. You can even make them so large, they run off the edge of the page, a technique called bleeding the image.

Click the photo to activate its handles. Drag the upper-left handle up and off the page into the gray area.

Some of the image will be trimmed at the edge and top.

Enlarging a photo this much creates a nice effect, making the image more dynamic, but leaving lots of white space for text.

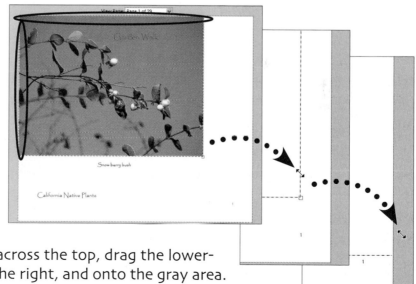

To bleed the image all across the top, drag the lower-right handle down, to the right, and onto the gray area.

lay out one photo (cont.)

Your photo is now large and dramatic, but it also covers all the text. You need to adjust the photo position and move or modify some text elements.

Position the pointer over the photo, away from any text. Drag the photo up.

Moving the photo up reveals the footer and page number.

It's usually best to delete the header when you push a photo to the top of the page. Double-click the header.

The Header dialog opens. Select the text and press Backspace or Delete.

Click the Done button to close the dialog.

The text box stays on the page, but it no longer displays text. Nothing will print.

creating albums with flexible layouts

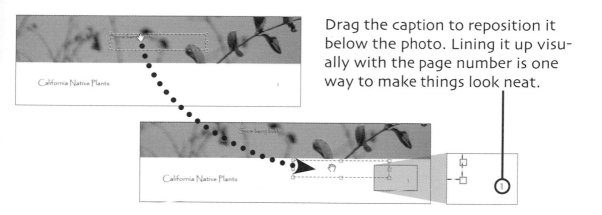

Drag the caption to reposition it below the photo. Lining it up visually with the page number is one way to make things look neat.

In the finished page the photo bleeds off the top and sides. All the crucial parts of the image fall inside the area bounded by the default header, footer, and page number. Whatever happens during trimming, this photo should still look OK.

lay out two photos

Click the next-page arrow to move to a page where you want two photos.

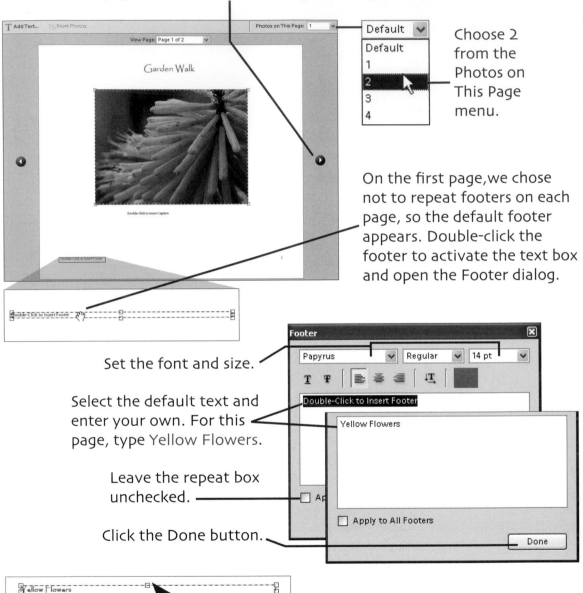

Choose 2 from the Photos on This Page menu.

On the first page, we chose not to repeat footers on each page, so the default footer appears. Double-click the footer to activate the text box and open the Footer dialog.

Set the font and size.

Select the default text and enter your own. For this page, type Yellow Flowers.

Leave the repeat box unchecked.

Click the Done button.

Enlarge the footer's text box. Drag the top handle up to reveal the footer text.

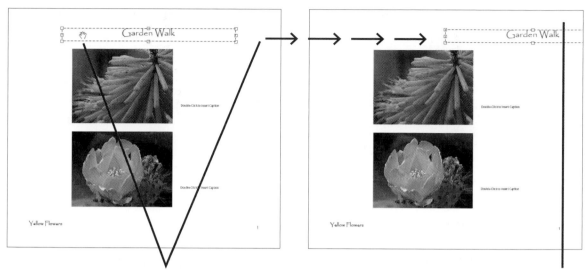

Move the header to make room for enlarging the photos. Click to select the header, but don't double-click. Press the → key to move the selected item 1-pixel to the right. Shift - → moves it 10 pixels.

Push the header to the right; visually line up the header's right edge with the page number's right edge.

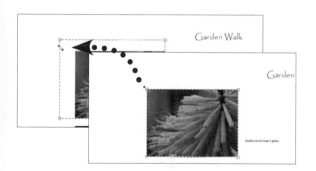

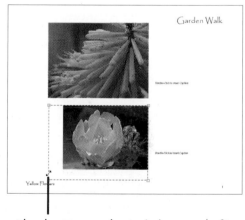

Drag the upper-left handle of the top photo outwards to enlarge the photo without running into the caption text box.

Drag the bottom photo's lower-left handle until it aligns (visually) with the top photo's left edge. The aspect ratio of these images is the same; enlarging them to the same width also makes them the same height

creating albums with flexible layouts

lay out two photos (cont.)

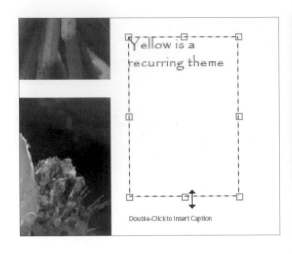

1 Double-click the top caption to open its Caption dialog.

2 Select the font, size, and color for your caption. Enter caption text. There's plenty of room to make a long caption to the right of the photos.

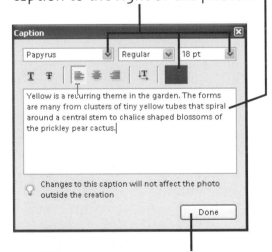

3 Click the Done button to close the dialog.

4 You need to open up the text box to show all of the large caption. But the other caption is in the way.

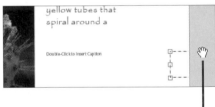

5 Drag that text box all the way off the page to delete it. Or drag it to a new position on the page.

6 Drag down to finish opening the caption text box.

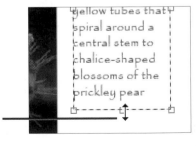

creating albums with flexible layouts

Layouts vary with the orientation of the photos involved. You've seen the layout for two landscape photos. Here are the other two-photo combinations.

You can always drag photos to a new position on the page.

If you just want to change the order in which the photos appear, however, it's better to return to Step 2 of the wizard and rearrange them there.

1 Click the Previous Step button.

3 Now click the Next Step button to return to Step 3 and the page you were on. The photo order has changed.

2 In Step 2, drag a photo to change the order. The yellow bar previews the new location.

lay out three photos

Click the next-page arrow to move to Page 3, where we'll lay out three photos.

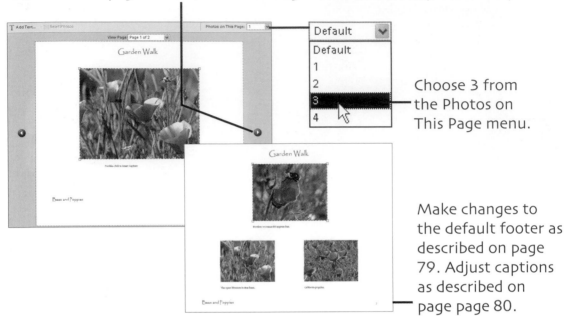

Choose 3 from the Photos on This Page menu.

Make changes to the default footer as described on page 79. Adjust captions as described on page page 80.

Use the objects on your page as alignment tools. Try putting the top photo's caption beside the photo instead of below it; line up the text with the photo.

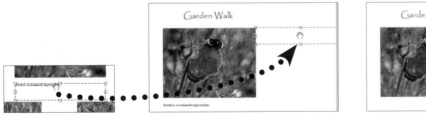

Click to select the caption.

Drag the caption to its new location. Position it so the selection marquee sits on the edge of the photo.

Use the arrow keys to move the caption away from the photo. A distance of 10 pixels looks good. Select the caption and press Shift-→ once.

creating albums with flexible layouts

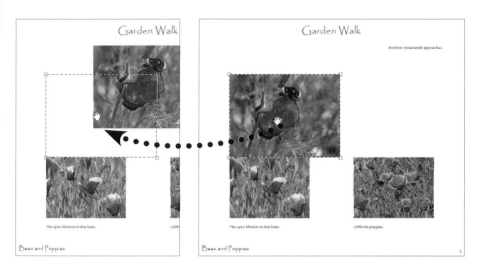

Use the same procedure to align photos. Drag the photo from the top of the page to sit right on top of the bottom-left photo.

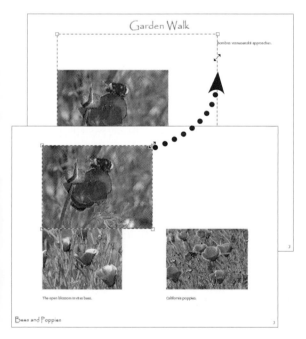

Drag the upper-right handle up and out until the edge of the photo's selection marquee meets the caption

You've enlarged the photo and preserved the original spacing on the right side of photo. Since you know that space is going to print safely, you can add display text there later.

creating albums with flexible layouts

lay out three photos (cont.)

With the photos lined up, try shrinking the smaller one even more. Click the photo to select it.

Drag the upper-right handle inward.

Repeat the process with the smaller photo on the right to match its size to the photo on the left visually.

Drag the right-hand photo closer to the one on the left.

Select the caption and press ← to move the caption to the left.

If you have trouble visually matching the photos when there's space between them, position one on top of the other, resize to match, then select one and use the arrow keys to position it.

creating albums with flexible layouts

You can add new text boxes to create display type. When you do, you may want to get rid of the individual captions because they look too cluttered.

Click the caption text to activate its text box. Drag the box completely off the page. Make sure that the resize handles no longer appear in the white area.

Click the Add Text button.

The Album Creation wizard puts new text boxes at the top of the page, right in the middle. Double-click the new text to open the Text dialog.

Choose the text attributes and enter your text.

Click Done to close the dialog.

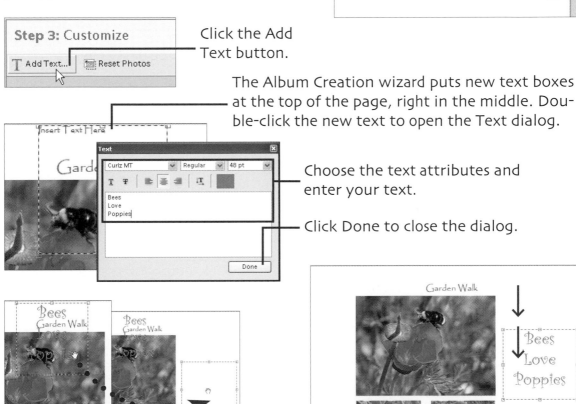

Drag the text box to the area where you want display text.

With the display text selected, use the arrow keys to position it.

lay out four photos

A four-photo page gives you lots of material to play with. Try different arrangements and sizes for your photos. To help line things up, you can create guidelines from text. You'll throw these guides away when you're done arranging.

Use the View Page menu to move to page 4 where we want to lay out four photos.

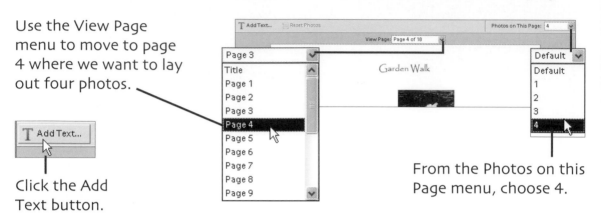

Click the Add Text button.

From the Photos on this Page menu, choose 4.

The Album Creation wizard places a text box on the page.

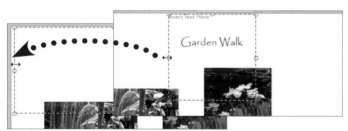

Drag the handle on the left side of the text box to the left edge of the page.

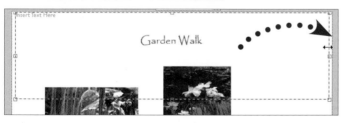

Drag the handle on the right side of the text box out to the right edge of the page.

Drag the bottom handle up to make a narrow box. Don't let the guideline text box overlap the header's box. Then double-click the text to open the Text dialog.

creating albums with flexible layouts

In the Text dialog, choose a sans serif font if you have one.

Choose a color that looks like a guide, say, bright green.

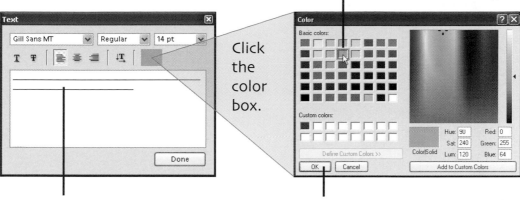

Click the color box.

To create a horizontal line, type underscore characters (Shift-–).

Click OK to close the Color dialog.

To create a vertical guide, select horizontal text.

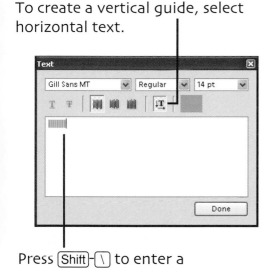

Press Shift-\ to enter a series of pipe characters (|). You could also use lowercase l's (l).

Position the Text dialog so that you can see the text box and watch the line grow as you type each character.

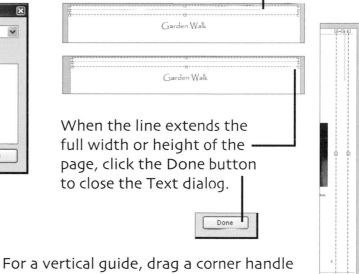

Garden Walk

Garden Walk

When the line extends the full width or height of the page, click the Done button to close the Text dialog.

Done

For a vertical guide, drag a corner handle to make the text box tall and thin.

creating albums with flexible layouts

lay out four photos (cont.)

When you move and resize photos to make a more creative layout the captions can seem to clutter the page. To remove the captions, drag them off the page and into the gray area.

For variety on a four-photo page, balance three small photos against a large one.

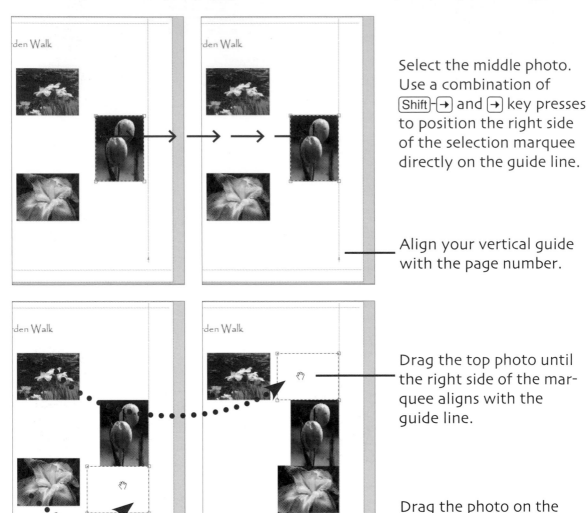

Select the middle photo. Use a combination of Shift-→ and → key presses to position the right side of the selection marquee directly on the guide line.

Align your vertical guide with the page number.

Drag the top photo until the right side of the marquee aligns with the guide line.

Drag the photo on the bottom until the right side of the marquee aligns with the guide line.

creating albums with flexible layouts

Select the top photo. Press [Shift]-[↑] three times to create space between the top and middle photos.

Select the bottom photo. Press [Shift]-[↓] three times to create the same space between the photos.

Place text guide lines at the top and bottom edges of the small-photo stack.

Drag the upper-right handle outwards until it sits on your guide line to make the image even larger.

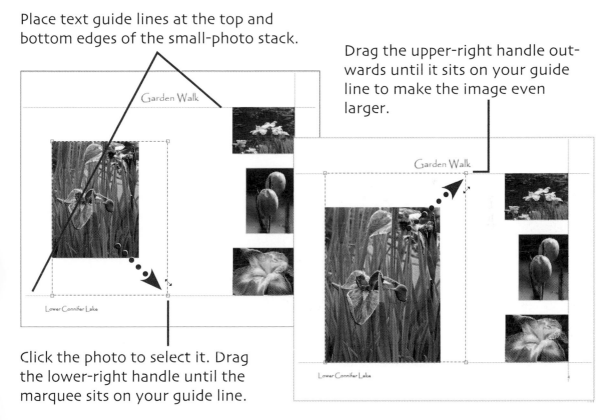

Click the photo to select it. Drag the lower-right handle until the marquee sits on your guide line.

creating albums with flexible layouts

lay out four photos (cont.)

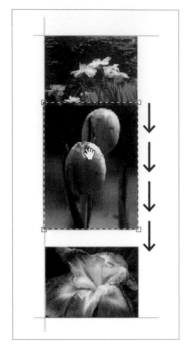

Align the guide line with the left edge of the top and bottom photos. Select the middle photo and drag its upper-left handle. Align the left side of the marquee with the guide line.

With the middle photo selected, press the ⬇ key (or Shift-⬇ keys) to move the middle photo down. Line up its lower edge to meet the top edge of the photo on the bottom.

Keep track of the number of presses. Then use the ⬆ key (or Shift-⬆ keys) to move the photo back up half that number of key presses. This centers the photo in the available space.

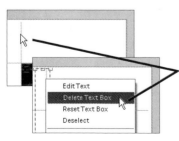

When you finish all alignments, you must remove any guides you created. These text elements will print in your album if you don't delete them. It's easiest to select the guide (instead of, say, the header) if you position the pointer over the guide near the edge of the page. Right-click the guide and choose Delete Text Box.

creating albums with flexible layouts

You can use additional text to create ornamental designs to accent your photos.

 Click the Add Text button.

The new text appears at the top of your page. Double-click it to open its Text dialog.

In the Text dialog, choose a pi font (one of the fonts that uses pictures instead of letters for each character).

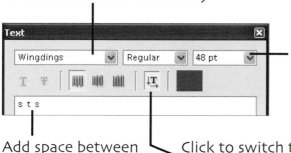

Increase the font size to make the ornaments bigger.

Add space between characters to separate ornamental elements.

Click to switch the orientation of your text from horizontal to vertical and vice versa.

Done — Click the Done button to close the Text dialog.

Use the aligning tricks you've learned to position the ornamental text. Don't go overboad adding doodads, but adding a little decoration is fun. Ornaments can tie images together, creating a theme for your book.

make blank pages

The Album Creation wizard always creates double-sided pages. But you can create one-sided pages by making a blank page. Why would you want to give up space for more photos? One reason to use a blank page is to prevent photos showing through on the opposite side of the page. This isn't a huge problem because Ofoto uses good quality paper. Still if the layouts differ on the front and back sides of a page, you can see shadows from the opposite side of the page. To prevent this, remove all of the photos and text elements from the page. (The exception here is the page number if you are using page numbers. The Album Creation wizard doesn't give you control over individual page numbers.)

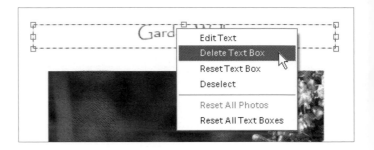

Right-click any text to access the contextual menu.

Choose Delete Text Box to remove it.

To remove photos, you must drag them off the page. (There's no contextual menu choice for it.) Drag the photo all the way off the white page area. Be sure that you no longer see the selection marquee and resize handles for the photo. The photo is still assigned to this page, but it won't print.

make text-only pages

Blank pages also give you room for lots of text. You can replicate the kind of text in columns that you find in books or magazines.

1 Click the Add Text button.

2 The wizard adds a new text box. Double-click the text to open its Text dialog.

3 Set options for your text. Select flush left for text alignment.

4 Enter the text you want to have in your first column.

5 Use 5 spaces for paragraph indents. (The Tab key won't work as it would in a text editor.)

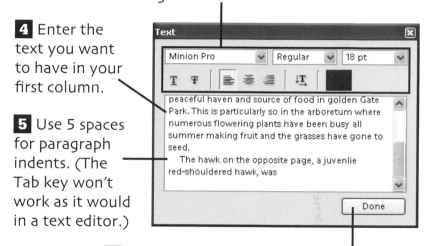

peaceful haven and source of food in golden Gate Park. This is particularly so in the arboretum where numerous flowering plants have been busy all summer making fruit and the grasses have gone to seed.

The hawk on the opposite page, a juvenlie red-shouldered hawk, was

6 Click the done button to close the dialog.

8 Drag a corner handle to resize the text box and display all the text.

7 Drag the text to the left side of the page.

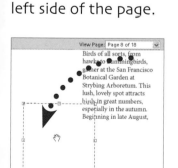

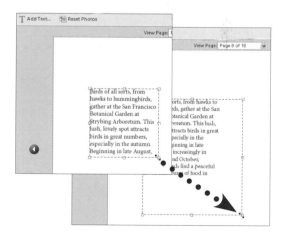

make text-only pages

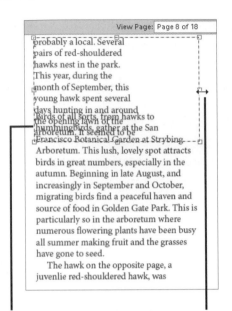

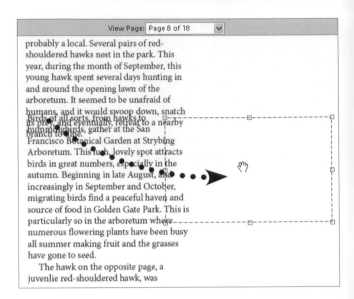

Create a second column. Move it to overlap the first, aligning both columns on the left. Drag one of the right-side resize handles to the right until the second column matches the first column's width.

Drag the second column. Place it to the right of the first. Let the text overlap.

Press the [→] (or [Shift]-[→]) key to move the column to the right, keeping it aligned.

Using the [↓] (or [Shift]-[↓]) keys, move the second column to align lines of text.

Birds of all sorts, from hawks to hummingbirds, gather at the San Francisco Botanical Garden at Strybing Arboretum. This lush, lovely spot attracts birds in great numbers, especially in the autumn. Beginning in late August, and increasingly in September and October, migrating birds find a peaceful haven and source of food in Golden Gate Park. This is particularly so in the arboretum where numerous flowering plants have been busy all summer making fruit and the grasses have gone to seed.

　The hawk on the opposite page, a juvenlie red-shouldered hawk, was

probably a local. Several pairs of red-shouldered hawks nest in the park. This year, during the month of September, this young hawk spent several days hunting in and around the opening lawn of the arboretum. It seemed to be unafraid of humans, and it would swoop down, snatch its prey, and eventually, retreat to a nearby branch to dine.

The yellow-rumped warbler is a visitor. It spends its summers further north; when autumn comes it heads south andmay spend the entire winter in the Bay Area.

fix page numbers

The Album Creation wizard creates inappropriate footers and page numbers for a bound book. In a bound album, the title page—a right-hand page—is really the book's first page, but the wizard doesn't number it. The wizard starts numbering with 1 on the first left-hand page. Odd numbers wind up on left-hand pages, evens on the right. Footers always appear in the lower-left corner of a page, page numbers in the lower-right corner. In a professionally designed book, on left-hand pages the numbers are even and appear in the lower-left corner. You can't edit the default page numbers in the Album Creation wizard, but you can add your own as additional text. You must then remove the default numbers.

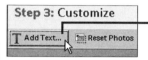

1 To fix page numbers and footers on left-hand pages, in Step 3, click the Add Text button. The Text dialog appears.

2 Choose a font family, size, and color. I like larger numbers; 24-point is huge, but it's easier to see in these examples.

Choose to align on the left. (For right-hand pages, choose align right.)

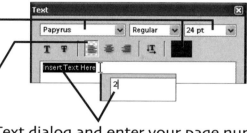

3 Select the default text in the Text dialog and enter your page number.

4 Click Done to close the dialog.

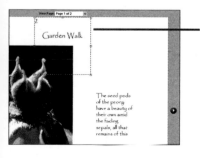

By default the wizard centers the additional text box at the top of the page.

5 Select the text and position the pointer over a corner resize handle. Drag to resize the box to show just the number.

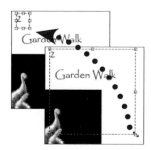

fix page numbers (cont.)

6 Position the pointer over the text box; drag the box until it covers the default page number.

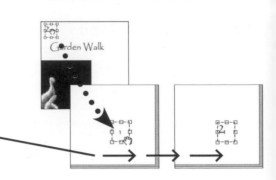

7 Click the box again to make sure it's selected, then use the arrow keys to align your number with the default number.

8 Press Shift-← or ← to move your selected page number to align with the left side of the footer.

9 Now select the footer, press Shift-→ and/ or → to move the footer to align with the default page number.

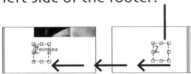 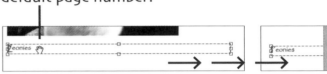

To fix page numbers and footers on right-hand pages, repeat Steps 1 through 7 of this task. The footer is already in the correct spot; you can skip Steps 8 and 9.

It's time to remove the default numbers. You must return to Step 1 of the wizard.

10 In the Step 3 page of the wizard, click Previous Step twice to return to the wizard's Step 1 page.

11 In Step 1, under Options, deselect the Page Numbers check box.

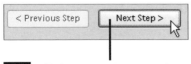 

12 Click Next Step twice to return to the Step 3 page.

The default page numbers are gone, leaving your numbers and repositioned footers.

creating albums with flexible layouts

do a critical review

When you finish laying out your entire album, you should review your pages.

Select Title from the View Page menu to jump to the beginning of the album.

When you move to a new page the wizard selects a photo.

Click the Next Page arrow to view each page in turn.

Right-click the photo; choose Deselect to hide the distracting marquee.

Give each page a critical review. Use your editor's eye to check for spelling mistakes in text. Double-click any text with typos to reopen its text-entry dialog to correct your mistake.

do a critical review (cont.)

Check that alignment of photos is precise. Use any of the techniques from this chapter to fine-tune your layout.

If you find a page where you wish you could start the layout over, don't despair.

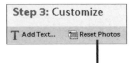

To restore photo defaults, click the Reset Photos button. Photos return to their default size and location on the page.

To restore default positions for text boxes (or photos), right-click anywhere on the page. Choose the items to restore from the contextual menu.

If you've deleted or moved any default text elements (headers, footers, photo captions), review those elements carefully. Moving back and forth between Step 3 and earlier steps (for example, to add more photos or change photo order in Step 2), sometimes restores those elements to their default positions. If you wanted to delete one of those elements, you may need to remove it again.

creating albums with flexible layouts

create PDF files

PDF files make excellent proofing tools. They allow you to see your pages unobstructed by the Album Creation wizard's interface. A really big plus is that you can view both pages of a spread simultaneously in a PDF. You can turn your album into a PDF in Step 5 of the Album Creation wizard. Be sure to save your album following the procedure outlined in Chapter 4: save and print (see pages 69 and 70) Then reopen your album and move to Step 5 of the wizard.

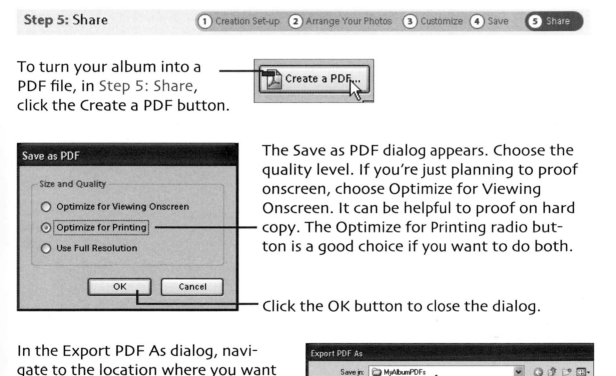

Step 5: Share   ① Creation Set-up ② Arrange Your Photos ③ Customize ④ Save ⑤ Share

To turn your album into a PDF file, in Step 5: Share, click the Create a PDF button.

The Save as PDF dialog appears. Choose the quality level. If you're just planning to proof onscreen, choose Optimize for Viewing Onscreen. It can be helpful to proof on hard copy. The Optimize for Printing radio button is a good choice if you want to do both.

Click the OK button to close the dialog.

In the Export PDF As dialog, navigate to the location where you want to keep your album PDFs.

Choose PDFs (*.pdf) as the file type.

Click Save.

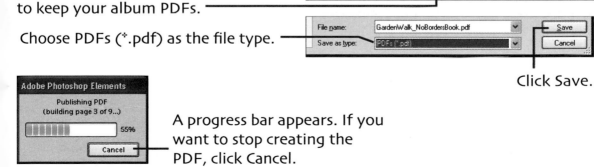

A progress bar appears. If you want to stop creating the PDF, click Cancel.

create PDF files (cont.)

To begin proofing right away, click Yes to open the PDF.

The PDF opens in Adobe Reader (when you installed Elements originally, it installed Reader 6.0 for you if you didn't already have it installed on your PC).

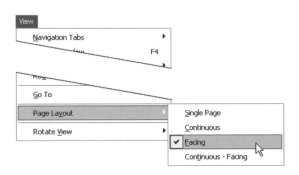

Choose View > Page Layout > Facing (or Continuous Facing) to see both pages of a spread at once. Viewing facing pages helps you judge how well the photos you selected go together and how your layout is working.

Reader's zoom tools let you view pages at various sizes.

Click the minus button to make pages smaller.

Click the plus button to make pages larger.

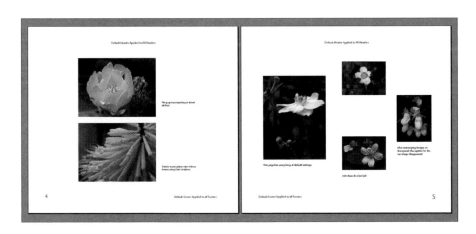

Now you see what an open album page looks like with the photos you've chosen for this spread.

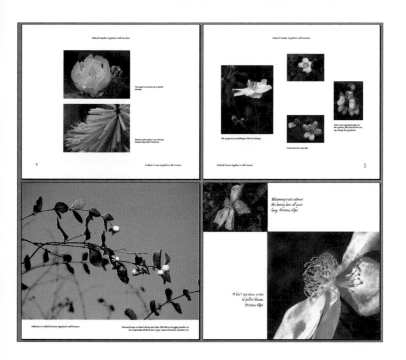

Zoom out more and you can see multiple spreads simultaneously.

Zoom out far enough and you can even see tiny thumbnails of the entire album to get a sense of the flow of images through the book.

A printed copy of an album makes a great proofing tool. Mark up the paper copy with corrections and any ideas for layout changes. You can print directly from the Album Creation wizard (as in Chapter 4) or print the PDF from Adobe Reader. Make corrections in Elements' Album Creation wizard then make a new PDF to proof. Repeat till you're satisfied with your album. Then order it (see Chapter 6).

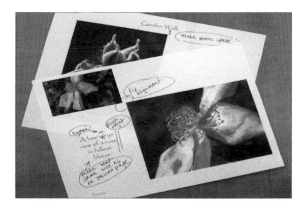

creating albums with flexible layouts

extra bits

choose a flexible album p. 74

- Photos with white or light edges, say a light sky, look odd in albums that don't use borders. Your eye can't tell where the photo stops and the page begins. Use the graphics tools in Editor's Standard Edit mode to add a thin outline or border to such photos.

know the print area p. 77

- When deciding whether to go outside the imaginary box formed by the header, footer, and page number, consider the importance of the item you're placing in the unpredictable zone. Placing text boxes near the right or left edge of the page is especially risky.

adjust captions p. 80

- Page 1 is the first page that has captions, so it makes sense to learn about adjusting captions now. For the rest of your album, however, you should hold off entering captions until you're certain you like the order, position, and size of your photos for each page. Switching the photo order after creating captions and other text elements could force you to redo text changes.

lay out one photo p. 81

- If you like full-page photos that bleed off the page, check out the Full Bleed Book album style. In its default layout, single photos fill the page, bleeding on all sides.

- When a resized photo covers a text element, you can choose to leave the text element in place. (A header that winds up in a section of blue sky, might look OK, where a header in a tangle of branches might not). Text elements always print over photos. You might want to adjust the text color, make it lighter to print over a dark photo or vice versa so that it stands out more in print.

- If you want complete freedom in creating layouts, use Editor's Standard Edit mode tools to create a single file for each album page. Set the document size to 8.5 by 11 inches for print-it-yourself album pages; 10.25 by 9 inches for photobooks. Combine photos, text, and graphic elements any way you want. You might, for example, place a dozen small snapshots on a page, yearbook fashion. Then import those files as the "photos" for your album. The Full Bleed Book style, was created specifically to facilitate this type of layout.

lay out two photos p. 84

- Using the arrow keys to move objects in albums can be tricky. Even when the selection marquee appears around an item the Album Creation wizard may not realize that item is selected. If you press the arrow keys and your selected object doesn't move (you may see buttons and menus highlighting instead), the wizard isn't recognizing your selection. It's safest to click the object you want to move, pause, then click again before pressing the arrow keys.

lay out four photos p. 92

- When creating color text, you can make darker or lighter versions of default colors. Drag the slider (next to the color space) up for lighter colors, down for darker.

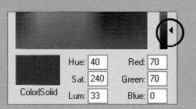

make text-only pages p. 99

- Album text boxes handle just one font and one size at a time. To combine text of different sizes (for a decorative capital, for example), use separate text boxes aligned to look like one paragraph. Click the Add Text button. In the Text dialog, choose a larger font size than in the paragraph; use the same font or a different one. Type the first letter of the paragraph and click Done. Resize the text box to fit closely around the letter. Double-click the paragraph where you want the large capital. In the Text dialog that opens, select the first letter of the paragraph and replace it with spaces to make room for the large capital; then click Done. Drag the large-letter text box over the paragraph. Position the text boxes so the large letter fits on the first line of the paragraph.

> Birds of all sort, from hawks to hummingbirds, gather at the San Francisco Botanical Garden at Strybing Arboretum. This lush, lovely spot attracts birds in great numbers,

> Birds of all sort, from hawks to hummingbirds, gather at the San Francisco Botanical Garden at Strybing Arboretum. This lush, lovely spot attracts birds in great numbers,

- To improve line breaks, double-click the text to open the Text dialog. Click between characters and type in a hyphen. Click the

creating albums with flexible layouts

extra bits

make text-only pages (cont.)

Done button. Resize the text box so the hyphen falls at the end of the line.

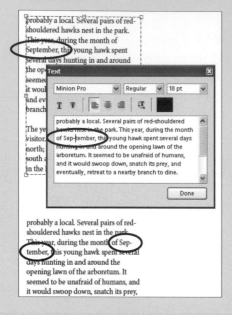

fix page numbers p. 101

- Most albums don't need numbered pages. You can simply remove the default page numbers. Skip task Steps 1 through 9; just follow Steps 10 through 12.

do a critical review p. 103

- No matter how carefully you edited your photos before creating your album, you're likely to see something else you'd like to

fix when you start reviewing your album pages. Unfortunately, if you edit the photos that you've placed in the album, you risk corrupting the album and losing all your work. To avoid that problem, return to Step 2 in the Album Creation wizard. Select the photo you'd like to edit and click the Remove Photo button at the top of the work area. Click the Close icon to exit the wizard. A dialog opens asking if you want to save changes. Click the Yes button; the wizard saves your album. You can now open your photo in Editor and make any needed changes. Return to Organizer's Photo Browser; double-click the album thumbnail to open your album; the wizard takes you to Step 3. Click the Previous Step button to move back to Step 2. Click the Add Photos button to reimport the edited photo. The wizard puts the photo at the end of your album. You'll need to drag the photo back to its proper place in the work area. Then click the Next Step button to move on to Step 3, where you can review each page again. The corrected photo should appear in place in your layout just fine. If necessary, make any further adjustments to your layout.

6. ordering hardcover photobooks

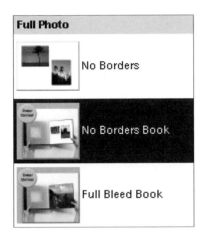

In September of 2004, Adobe Systems and Eastman Kodak teamed up to provide Elements users with new ways to share photos, both online and in print. This collaboration is officialy known as Adobe Photoshop Services, Provided by Ofoto. Ofoto is Kodak's online photo subsidiary. I'll be referring to it as Adobe Photoshop Services (APS) and Ofoto for the rest of this book.

One of the APS products you can order is a printed hardcover book starring your very own photos. Choose one of the album styles that bears a yellow Order Online medallion, to create an album that you can order as a hardcover book.

Album covers come in a variety of materials, the most expensive being leather. A window cut out of the front cover lets part of the first page show through. (The Book album styles help you place a photo directly below this window, so that the image shows through when the cover is closed.)

The hardcover books measure 10.25 by 9 inches. The interior pages are fairly heavy weight, archival quality, coated stock—that is, fairly thick paper with a low acid content (so it will last a long time) and a smooth glossy finish. The smallest photobook you can order contains 20 pages (10 sheets of paper, printed on both sides). Once you've filled those 20 pages, you can add more pages, two at a time, up to the maximum of 40 pages.

start the order process

To start the order process, in Step 5: Share of the Album Creation wizard, click the Order Online button.

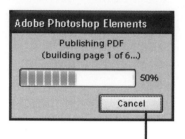

The wizard creates a Portable Document Format (PDF) file of your album. To stop the process click Cancel.

The first time you use Adobe Photoshop Services on your computer, whether to order prints, share photos online, or order an album, you'll see a Welcome page. If your first experience with APS is ordering an album, the Welcome page appears just after the wizard creates the PDF file.

Click the Sign In link to log in to an existing account (see page 114).

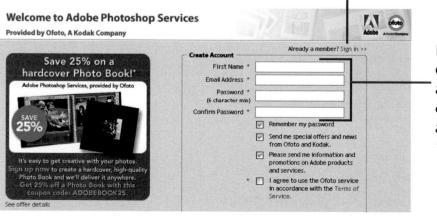

Enter your name, email address, and a password to start creating a new account (see page 113).

ordering hardcover photobooks

set up your account

Create Accounts

To order a photobook, you need an APS or Ofoto account. The first time you use APS, the Create Account fields appear on the Welcome page. You can also access the Create Account fields by clicking the Change link in Step 1 (see page 114).

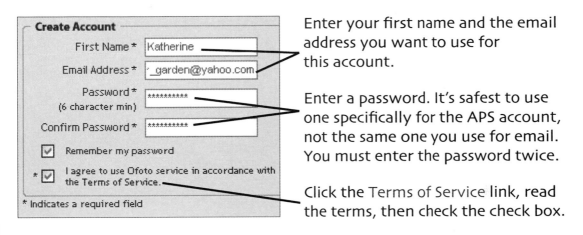

Enter your first name and the email address you want to use for this account.

Enter a password. It's safest to use one specifically for the APS account, not the same one you use for email. You must enter the password twice.

Click the Terms of Service link, read the terms, then check the check box.

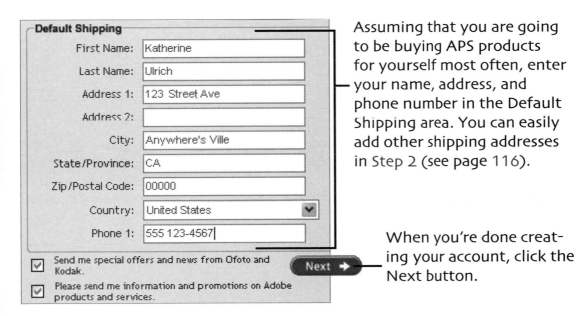

Assuming that you are going to be buying APS products for yourself most often, enter your name, address, and phone number in the Default Shipping area. You can easily add other shipping addresses in Step 2 (see page 116).

When you're done creating your account, click the Next button.

log in to your account

Order Photobook

Step: ① Customize   ② Recipients   ③ Summary   ④ Billing   ⑤ Upload   ⑥ Confirmation

The Order Photobook wizard guides you through the ordering process.

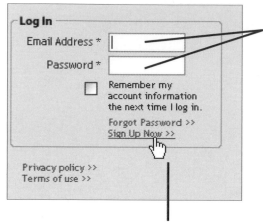

On the Step 1: Customize page, if you already have an APS or Ofoto account you just need to log in. Enter the email address and password you used to set up the account.

If you want to set up a new APS account, click the Sign Up Now link to go to the Create Accounts page (described on page 113).

Then click the Next button. APS verifies your account information and returns you to Step 1.

If you've already used Elements 3.0 to share photos online or order prints, you've already set up an APS account. If you chose to remember your password, the log-in segment doesn't appear in Step 1. Instead, the account holder's first name appears as the active account at the top of the page.

To change the account, click the Change link to go to the Create Account page.

step 1: customize

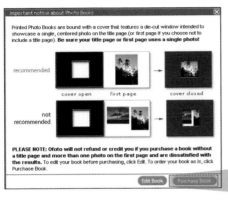

Before you start the actual order process, the wizard warns you about how the die-cut cover and title page work together. We've used a default title page to ensure that the image fits the window. Go ahead and click the Purchase Book button.

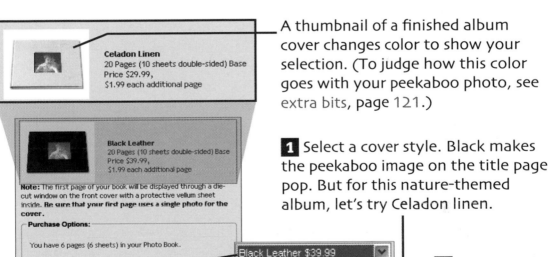

A thumbnail of a finished album cover changes color to show your selection. (To judge how this color goes with your peekaboo photo, see extra bits, page 121.)

1 Select a cover style. Black makes the peekaboo image on the title page pop. But for this nature-themed album, let's try Celadon linen.

3 To continue your order, click the Next button.

2 Enter the number of albums you want to order.

step 2: recipients

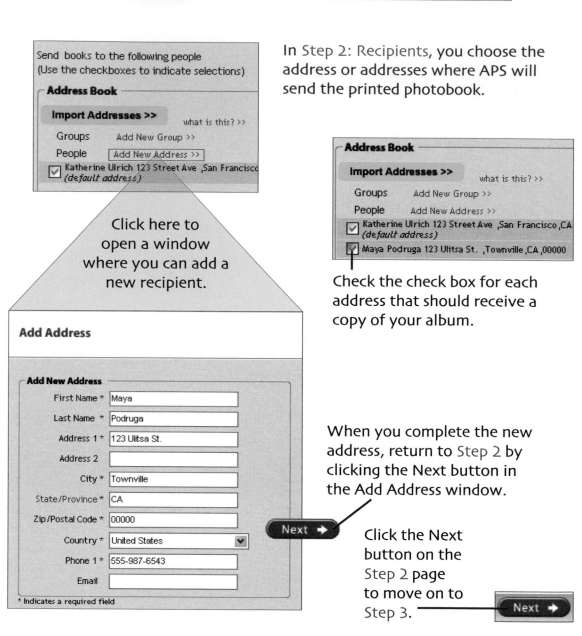

Order Photobook

Step: ① Customize ❷ Recipients ③ Summary ④ Billing ⑤ Upload ⑥ Confirmation

Send books to the following people
(Use the checkboxes to indicate selections)

Address Book

Import Addresses >>   what is this? >>

Groups   Add New Group >>

People   Add New Address >>

☑ Katherine Ulrich 123 Street Ave ,San Francisco
(default address)

In Step 2: Recipients, you choose the address or addresses where APS will send the printed photobook.

Address Book

Import Addresses >>   what is this? >>

Groups   Add New Group >>

People   Add New Address >>

☑ Katherine Ulrich 123 Street Ave ,San Francisco ,CA
(default address)

☑ Maya Podruga 123 Ulitsa St. ,Townville ,CA ,00000

Check the check box for each address that should receive a copy of your album.

Click here to open a window where you can add a new recipient.

Add Address

Add New Address

First Name *	Maya
Last Name *	Podruga
Address 1 *	123 Ulitsa St.
Address 2	
City *	Townville
State/Province *	CA
Zip/Postal Code *	00000
Country *	United States
Phone 1 *	555-987-6543
Email	

* Indicates a required field

When you complete the new address, return to Step 2 by clicking the Next button in the Add Address window.

Next ➔

Click the Next button on the Step 2 page to move on to Step 3.

Next ➔

step 3: summary

Order Photobook

Step: ① Customize ② Recipients ❸ Summary ④ Billing ⑤ Upload ⑥ Confirmation

In Step 3: Summary, you verify the details of your order, choose a shipping method, and apply any discounts you may have received from Adobe Photoshop Services or Ofoto.

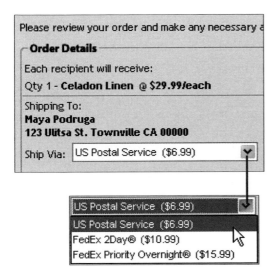

APS offers shipping by U.S. mail and FedEx. Shipments originate from the West Coast. Choose your preferred shipping method from the drop-down menu.

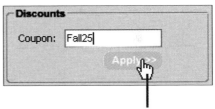

Enter any discount codes you have. You must click the Apply button to receive the credit. The Order Summary recalculates.

Click the Next button to continue the ordering process.

ordering hardcover photobooks

step 4: billing

Order Photobook

Step: ① Customize ② Recipients ③ Summary **④ Billing** ⑤ Upload ⑥ Confirmation

In Step 4:Billing, you provide credit card information to pay for your order.

Select your credit card type.

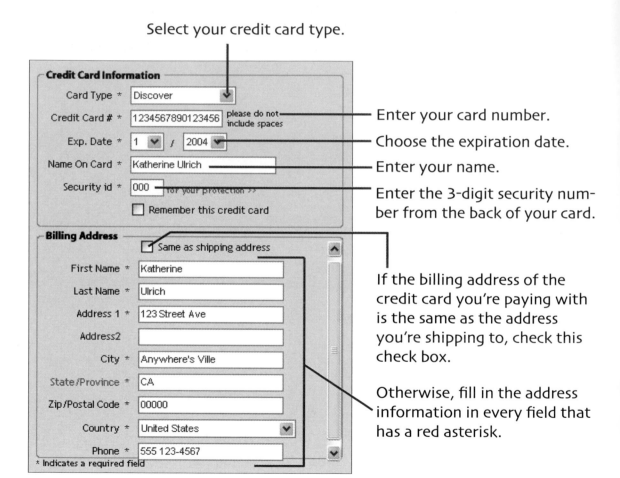

Enter your card number.

Choose the expiration date.

Enter your name.

Enter the 3-digit security number from the back of your card.

If the billing address of the credit card you're paying with is the same as the address you're shipping to, check this check box.

Otherwise, fill in the address information in every field that has a red asterisk.

Double-check all your billing information. Make any needed corrections. Then click the Place Order button to send your order request to APS/Ofoto.

step 5: upload

Order Photobook

Step: ① Customize ② Recipients ③ Summary ④ Billing ⑤ Upload ⑥ Confirmation

In Step 5: Upload, a progress bar tracks how much of your album has been sent to Adobe Photoshop Services/Ofoto. The file being uploaded is actually the PDF file of your album, not the individual images within it. Still, depending on how many pages and photos you've used in your album, the file can be large. If you are using a dial-up connection, you may want to carry out your order session when you have time to be online for a bit.

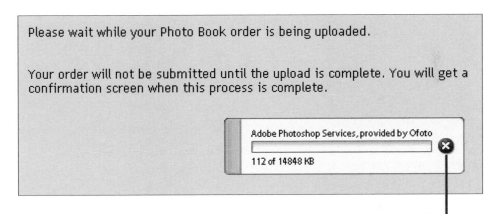

Please wait while your Photo Book order is being uploaded.

Your order will not be submitted until the upload is complete. You will get a confirmation screen when this process is complete.

Adobe Photoshop Services, provided by Ofoto

112 of 14848 KB

To cancel the upload process, click the Close button.

There is no Next button for this step. When the upload is finished you move directly to Step 6.

step 6: confirmation

Order Photobook
Confirmation

The step numbers disappear from the top of the Order Photobook wizard, but this is Step 6: Confirmation. In addition to this summary of your completed order, you'll receive email letting you know that APS/Ofoto has received the order. You'll receive another email when the order ships.

Print this Confirmation >>

Order Confirmation

Order Number: 76163478406

Thank you for your order Katherine. A confirmation email will be sent to walker_garden@yahoo.com.

To print a copy of this confirmation screen, click the Print button.

You can use your order number to track your purchase at the Ofoto website.

Shipping to

Katherine Ulrich
123 Street Ave
Anywhere's Ville, CA 00000

Order Summary

Show Current Promotion >>

Qty	Item	Price
1 -	Celadon Linen	$29.99
	Shipping & Handling	$6.99
	Taxes	$1.87
	Total	**$38.85**

Go to your member account
http://www.adobe.ofoto.com

To open a browser window showing the Ofoto website, click the active link. Once at the Ofoto site, you can enter your account and check the status of your order.

To exit the order process, click the Done button. The Order Photobook wizard closes, and you return to the Album Creation wizard at Step 5: Share.

ordering hardcover photobooks

extra bits

start the order process p. 112

- If your album contains fewer pages than the 20-page minimum-size album, the Order Photobook wizard warns you of that fact. You can stop the ordering process and return to the Album Creation wizard to edit your album.

set up your account p. 113

- Sign up to learn about discounts and special offers by checking the Send Me Special Offers . . . check box below the Default Shipping section when you create your account. (Or you can Choose Edit > Preferences > Services and check the Show Notifications about Adobe Promotions check box in the Updates section.) In Organizer, click the Notifications icon to see any new APS offers.

step 1: customize p. 115

- After you pick a cover, position the Order Photobook window so that you can see the Album Creation window and Order Photobook window (with the title-page photo) simultaneously. If you've set both wizards to fill the screen (using the Maximize icon) you will need to restore the Order Photobook wizard to a resizable window (click the Restore icon in the upper-right corner of the window). You can get a rough idea of how the cover color goes with your title-page photo.

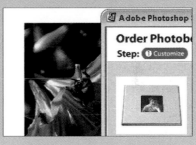

extra bits

step 3: summary p. 117

- Check the Ofoto web site (www.ofoto.com) to find any discounts or sales that are currently available.

- APS/Ofoto sometimes ships coupons with one finished order good for discounts on the next.

index

index

index

index

index

index

index

index

index

titles
    photo album, 69
    placeholder, 65
tonal adjustments, 36
Trash icon, 44
trimming photos. See
    cropping photos

Undo button, 45
Unsharp Mask filter, 54
Update Creations button, 56

version sets, 25, 33, 50–51
vertical guides, 93–94
video-card requirements for
    Elements, 2

warning triangle, 68
Watch folders, 8
website for Ofoto, 120
websites, 72, 120, 122
Welcome Screen, 5
windows, resizing, 43
work area, 43

![z]

zoom tools, 29, 46, 106–107